Poised for Peak
Performance in Healthcare

Poised for Peak Performance in Healthcare

A Practical Approach to Execute Expense Reduction and Revenue Enhancement Initiatives

By
Ali Birjandi, MBA, MHA, SSBB, CPHIMS

A PRODUCTIVITY PRESS BOOK

Routledge
Taylor & Francis Group
711 Third Avenue, New York, NY 10017
© 2018 by Taylor & Francis Group, LLC
CRC Press is an imprint of Taylor & Francis Group, an Informa business

No claim to original U.S. Government works

Printed on acid-free paper

International Standard Book Number-13: 978-1-138-03966-7 (Paperback)
International Standard Book Number-13: 978-1-138-03974-2 (Hardback)
International Standard Book Number-13: 978-1-315-17566-9 (eBook)

Library of Congress Cataloging-in-Publication Data

Names: Birjandi, Ali, author.
Title: Poised for peak performance in healthcare : a practical approach to execute expense reduction and revenue enhancement initiatives / Ali Birjandi.
Description: Boca Raton : Taylor & Francis, 2018. | Includes bibliographical references and index.
Identifiers: LCCN 2017053387 (print) | LCCN 2017055459 (ebook) | ISBN 9781315175669 (ebook) | ISBN 9781138039667 (pbk. : alk. paper) | ISBN 9781138039742 (hardback : alk. paper)
Subjects: | MESH: Practice Management | Delivery of Health Care--organization & administration | Delivery of Health Care--economics
Classification: LCC RA971.3 (ebook) | LCC RA971.3 (print) | NLM W 80 | DDC 362.1068--dc23
LC record available at https://lccn.loc.gov/2017053387

Visit the Taylor & Francis Web site at
http://www.taylorandfrancis.com

and the CRC Press Web site at
http://www.crcpress.com

To my wife, Kathleen, for all of the support she has given me throughout this effort. Most of this work was done on weekends, nights, while on vacation, and other times inconvenient to my family. And to my sons, Cameron, Jordan, and Aidan, who are the inspiration in my life.

CONTENTS

Preface

The human determination for longevity and good health is deeply rooted in our genetic code for survival. It is this human drive that compels many of us to go into healthcare and serve our communities. Unfortunately, our ability to provide access to cost-effective care has diminished every year for the past three decades. This is a direct result of our inability to change quickly in an era of high competition and lower reimbursements. My motivation in writing this book was based on the sincere desire to advance the evolution of healthcare through best practices for all communities.

At 18% of GDP, the US healthcare system is, without rival, the most expensive in the world. For three decades, our greatest leaders have been working to improve cost, quality, and service, without much success. Although many organizations have learned to do well, some still do not know the basic principles that lead to high performance. As pressures from regulatory agencies, consumers, and competition heat up in the next decade, many organizations will find themselves desperate for practical solutions for their very survival.

This book is a culmination of my 25 years of healthcare Performance Improvement (PI) experience in top-performing systems across the United States, and my attempt to disseminate operational best practices by sharing what has worked and what has not. It is a step-by-step "how to" book to help set up basic programs around traditional expense reduction initiatives that can double or triple the margin for your organization.

In just 100 days, I believe this book can help struggling organizations improve labor, supplies, access, revenue cycle, and length of stay. By developing these systems through the continuous quality improvement methodology, you can put into place a system that will generate millions perpetually into the future.

With the never-ending cycle of lower reimbursements and increased competition, it is my sincere hope that organizations can be better prepared for survival by adopting these best practices. The survival of healthcare institutions is not just good for the organization, but good for all Americans.

Acknowledgments

I would like to say thank you to the following individuals:

My late boss and mentor Ray Thompson for providing the support that gave me the opportunity to implement many of these innovative business models that have been developed over the years. Many of these innovative solutions and conceptual models could not have been implemented without a strong leader behind the Performance Improvement program.

Dr. Dror Paley for teaching me how we can always do more with less. His mentorship has been invaluable in creating a strong work ethic in the pursuit of one's passion and creating a new sense of inquisitiveness that keeps pushing me to experiment with new concepts and opportunities.

Michael Rowan for mentoring me on the practical application of healthcare change and the value of diversity in innovation and group thinking. His leadership allowed me to understand the fierce rate of change in healthcare that precipitated a practical approach to increase speed from concept to implementation in Performance Improvement.

How to Maximize the Value of This book

Great leaders see the world from an optimistic view and can see the good in everything. They have no reservations in seeing their own limitations and have little trouble bringing in the right talent to get the job done. They keep the vision simple, solutions practical, and are always open to doing things better. The premise of this book is based on this practical approach in defining our pathway into the next decade.

Set high standards: Going from good to great is a continuous quality improvement process. The premise of this book is that everything can be done better. In healthcare, we have been pulling the same levers for over 25 years to improve performance. Whether it involves Labor, Non-labor, or Length of Stay expenses, it is critical that we always reach for perfection. Many of the barriers in front of management are self-generated and have no basis in reality. When reading this book, think in terms of an undiminished yearning for perfection in the delivery of care.

Adapt and adjust: Although the goal of performance improvement in its primal sense strives to reduce variability, it is critical to know that today's organizations are as diverse as ever. Our differences are not just in our culture, but also in our processes, systems, and management. The methodologies in this book may require leaders to adapt and adjust these concepts into the existing models to produce the highest chance for success within their organizations. Be ready to adapt and adjust to get to the solution.

Speed is life: Healthcare is changing at an increasing rate. Performance improvement methodologies that previously required 6 months to design and implement are obsolete in today's environment. Practical solutions must be able to take flight in less than 100 days and often have to operate on limited data. Organizations that are able to rapidly change have a much higher chance of survival in the next decade. The infrastructure and governance process described in this book are practical in nature.

Redefine your paradigms: The future of healthcare requires new innovative approaches to traditional models of performance improvement. For innovation to occur, we need to think openly and understand clearly that we discriminate based on human nature. The future of healthcare requires big changes in short periods of time and this will require future leaders to elevate their concept of performance improvement to a more strategic and collaborative role.

Breaking down the value model: The value model consists of providing the highest quality of care with the best patient experience at the lowest cost. All three elements have to be in balance with each other to maximize value for the patient. The focus of this book is on the expense reduction portion of the equation.

About the Author

Ali Birjandi is a senior healthcare executive leader who develops and manages Performance Improvement (PI) programs to elevate organizations to their highest potential. He is a strong advocate for continuous improvement in the delivery of healthcare. To this end, he is continuously developing new strategies, tools, processes, and products to help organizations reach their maximum operational performance potential.

As the creator of the PI Hybrid methodology, Ali Birjandi has been a pioneer in developing practical approaches that use a disciplined program implementation methodology along with traditional process engineering tools. Although Ali is a guide and a consultant to senior leadership in the design and development of Performance Improvement programs, his preference is to be on the frontline where the innovation occurs.

A frequent speaker at national and international healthcare conferences, Ali Birjandi is a two-time recipient of the IBM Truven Advantage Award for Operational Excellence and Efficiency. He is also a member of ASQ, HIMSS, and SHS with certifications as a Six Sigma Master Black Belt and is a Certified Professional in the Health Information Management Systems Society.

Ali Birjandi has written multiple articles in various publications on a number of Performance Improvement topics, and is the co-author of the *Discharge Planning Handbook for Healthcare: Top 10 Secrets to Unlocking a New Revenue Pipeline*. He can be contacted at birjandi@yahoo.com.

KEY REQUIRED CHANGES IN THE DELIVERY MODEL

Chapter 1

Healthcare Drivers in the Next Decade

> America's health care system is neither healthy,
> caring, nor a system.
>
> **Walter Cronkite**

In 1996, when I was graduating from the University of Florida, the keynote speaker made a very profound statement in his speech that was to be the undercurrent of all the ensuing changes that were coming to healthcare. He said, "We all know that the healthcare system in the U.S. is the most expensive compared to the rest of the world. But what we don't know, is how little we are getting for that money." The concept of getting the most value for your money whether in healthcare, or anything for that matter, is fundamental. It goes beyond the traditional questions of socialized medicine versus free market, Democrat versus Republican, or the age-old question of whether healthcare is a right or a privilege. In this inherent assumption, getting the most from our resources is a universal concept that we should all cherish and strive for.

In 2010, the Organization for Economic Co-operation and Development (OECD) shared the per capita healthcare spending of the top 15 most developed nations around the world. The OECD is an international body that collects and analyzes data on various social and economic indicators. If any picture is worth a thousand words, this is it. It shows clearly how the United States outpaced the rest of the world in per capita spending at $7538 with the next closest country Norway at $5000. What this analysis does not show is that annual healthcare spending growth rates are also the highest in the United States. Not only is the US healthcare system the most expensive in the world, it is getting more expensive at a faster rate than everywhere else. See Exhibits 1.1 and 1.2.

The collective response from most politicians and industry leaders is that the best healthcare system in the world requires the most resources. This was a great explanation until the Commonwealth Fund came out with the National Scoreboard that performed an assessment to rank the best healthcare systems in the world. They ranked the top 11 countries in five categories: quality, access, efficiency, equity, and healthy lives. The results were astounding in that they showed the United

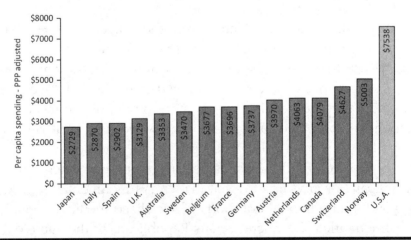

Exhibit 1.1   Graph indicating cost per capita spending by top 15 countries.

From: Organization for Economic Co-operation and Development (OECD) (2010), "OECD Health Data," OECD Health Statistics (database). doi: 10.1787/data-00350-en (accessed February 14, 2011).

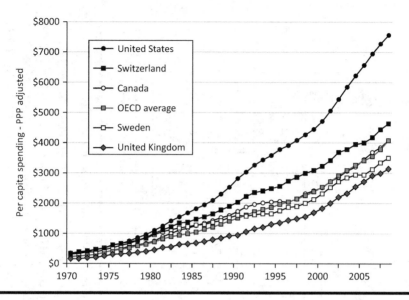

Exhibit 1.2   Per capita spending by top five countries from 1970 to 2010.

From: OECD (2010), "OECD Health Data," OECD Health Statistics (database). doi: 10.1787/data-00350-en (accessed February 14, 2011).

States in last place. These were universal measures that were used in some form or another by the leading industry agencies such as the IHI, Institute of Medicine (IOM), ASQ, TJC, and CMS to measure the value of healthcare. See Exhibit 1.3.

This should not have come as a surprise, as in 1999, the IOM put out a report that in essence verified the Health Fund data. The report was based on an analysis of multiple studies in the United States by a variety of organizations, and concluded that between 44,000 and 98,000 people die each year as a result of preventable medical errors. This was one of the first studies that would ultimately show that medical errors are the third leading cause of death in the United States just below heart disease and cancer. This statistic made healthcare organizations almost as dangerous as the diseases themselves.

With healthcare expenses approaching 18% of gross domestic product and outcomes below expectations, the current

Country rankings

| Top 2* |
| Middle |
| Bottom 2* |

	AUS	CAN	FRA	GER	NETH	NZ	NOR	SWE	SWIZ	UK	US
Overall ranking (2013)	4	10	9	5	5	7	7	3	2	1	11
Quality care	2	9	8	7	5	4	11	10	3	1	5
Effective care	4	7	9	6	5	2	11	10	8	1	3
Safe care	3	10	2	6	7	9	11	5	4	1	7
Coordinated care	4	8	9	10	5	2	7	11	3	1	6
Patient-centered care	5	8	10	7	3	6	11	9	2	1	4
Access	8	9	11	2	4	7	6	4	2	1	9
Cost-related problem	9	5	10	4	8	6	3	1	7	1	11
Timeliness of care	6	11	10	4	2	7	8	9	1	3	5
Efficiency	4	10	8	9	7	3	4	2	6	1	11
Equity	5	9	7	4	8	10	6	1	2	2	11
Healthy lives	4	8	1	7	5	9	6	2	3	10	11
Healthy expenditures/capita, 2011**	$3800	$4522	$4118	$4495	$5099	$3182	$5669	$3925	$5643	$3405	$8508

Exhibit 1.3   Commonwealth table showing the top 11 countries ranked in 5 categories of performance.

Notes: *Includes ties. **Expenditures shown in US dollar purchasing power parity (PPP); Australian dollar data are from 2010. (From calculations by The Commonwealth Fund based on 2011 International Health Policy Survey of Sicker Adults; 2012 International Health Policy Survey of Primary Care Physicians; 2013 International Health Policy Survey; Commonwealth Fund National Scorecard 2011; World Health Organization; and Organization for Economic Co-operation and Development, OECD Health Data, 2013 [Paris: OECD, November 2013].)*

system is due for an overhaul. Unfortunately, the current system is going to get worse before it gets better. New forces are accelerating the pace of change in healthcare. These forces have come in the form of regulatory, reimbursement, market, and consumer pressures. See Exhibit 1.4.

Healthcare is one of the most highly regulated industries in the United States. There are federal, state, county, and industry agencies that have significant influence and control over the day-to-day operations of healthcare organizations. These agencies control everything from reimbursement to licensing. The breadth of control reaches even day-to-day operational tasks such as staffing and the administration of drugs. Regulatory agencies have been very intrusive in dictating to providers how to operate within current and future models of healthcare. For this reason, change has been slow and erratic in the industry.

With expenses and consumption in healthcare increasing every year, reimbursements have been tightened to keep pace. The situation is confounded by the baby boomers slowly reaching retirement with increasing dependence on healthcare. With the government leading the charge to decrease reimbursements, other major payors have followed. These reductions have come in many forms, one of which is the increasing shift to pay-for-performance models. It is expected that, year

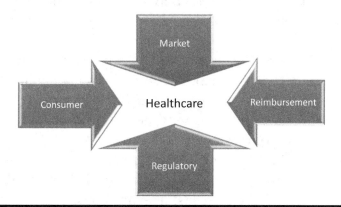

Exhibit 1.4   Four main sources of pressure on healthcare.

after year, the financial risk for providers will increase. Other mechanisms used to reduce reimbursements include creating narrow networks and allowing the market to compete for the best price.

As margins continue to thin, healthcare markets have been in flux as organizations vie to position themselves for survival. Market pressures have come from many directions. These include, but are not limited to, medical tourism from abroad, consolidation of medical practices, mergers and acquisitions, and free-standing emergency rooms. These market pressures have forced many organizations to consolidate for economies of scale, file for bankruptcy to fend off creditors, and affiliate to stay alive.

The last major impact on healthcare is driven by consumers. Traditionally, up until the last 20 years, this was almost never the case. As the burden of healthcare costs increasingly falls on the shoulders of patients, they in turn increasingly want to know how much their care costs and what they are paying for. The conversation that used to be about the treatment and the recommendation of the doctor has turned into "how much is this going to cost?" As deductibles and co-pays reach $10,000+, hospitals and physician practices are providing financial counselors and payment plans. In many cases, the patients are foregoing treatment because of unaffordability. As the burden increasingly falls on the shoulders of patients, we can expect greater scrutiny over service, quality, and costs.

As the healthcare system began to experience an inability to meet the growing demands of the US population, major payors such as CMS and BCBS were the first to react. With a new product dubbed "managed care," the payors attempted to shift the burden of risk toward the providers and consumers of healthcare. In this model, provider networks were tightened and reimbursements reduced with potentially higher volumes.

With lower reimbursements, healthcare leaders were quick to respond precipitously to keep the margins from falling.

Many CEOs and healthcare leaders focused on singular strategies such as superior quality, service excellence, or expense reduction strategies to develop a core competency to help drive the organization ahead of the pack.

Organizations seeing the growth of the Joint Commission, CMS, and payor quality metrics such as Core Measures pushed quality in every facet of healthcare. Quality became the mantra for not just the clinical aspect of care, but also things such as billing, registration, and marketing. Typical quality departments grew from small, 2–3 full-time equivalent (FTE) functions to large, 20–30 FTE departments overnight. Quality departments picked up many Performance Improvement (PI) methodologies, such as Quality Improvement Teams, used a watered-down version of the Six Sigma DMAIC model called Action Workouts, and treated every process as a quality issue.

In the early 2000s, there was a great push for service initiatives to break through the competitive barriers and create a differentiating factor among organizations. This was based on the premise that as fees were controlled by the insurers and quality was an expectation, it was service that would be the differentiating factor that would drive patient volumes. Overnight, programs such as the Studer Group's "Hardwiring Excellence" and Disney's "On-Stage, Off-Stage" became popular among many organizations. This was ultimately fueled by CMS incorporating patient experience into their hospital comparison program.

With payors decreasing reimbursements and consumers having to pay a larger portion of their medical bills, it soon became clear that with no margin there is no mission. Additionally, as provider expenses were growing at two to three times the inflation rate, organizations soon realized that none of this matters if it can't keep its doors open. As deductibles and co-pays were skyrocketing, many organizations developed aggressive tactics to collect from patients on the revenue side. Hence, in many cities the largest number of personal bankruptcies were due to medical bills.

The healthcare industry was quick to realize that the current system is much more complicated. Patients did not want to sacrifice any of these pillars of healthcare for another. For example, no one wants to be in a world-class emergency room and have to wait 6 hours to see a doctor. Likewise, no patient wants to go to hospitals that have low wait times, but high mortality rates or infectious disease issues. Increasingly, as healthcare shifts the financial burden onto them, patients want both quality and service at the lowest possible price. This combination of quality and service at the lowest cost is inherent in the "value proposition." In the future, organizations that can identify this optimized state for patients, payors, and providers will thrive. On this journey, many pioneering organizations started tracking basic organizational metrics through such tools as the balanced report card to show service, quality, and costs. CMS started using pay-for-performance to tie reimbursements to quality, service, and cost of care in a balanced view.

As market, consumer, reimbursement, and regulatory pressures grow year after year, provider margins are dropping at an increasing rate. Organizations have tried many countermeasures to adapt to the new environment. This includes, but is not limited to, strategies such as mergers, affiliations, physician alignment, expansion, and PI.

Increasingly, organizations have been looking to PI methodologies to help information, discipline, and execution become faster and stronger. Also known as management engineering, process re-engineering, or process transformation, PI is the vehicle that data-driven organizations will be using to outperform their competitors. PI functions have been expanding their role beyond expense reduction programs and further into clinical utilization, quality, and patient experience in the last decade. High-performing PI functions today typically manage labor expense reduction, non-labor expense reduction, revenue cycle, length of stay (LOS) reduction, patient experience, and zero harm. Although PI functions may have their own nuances across organizations, the output is to design systems and processes for operators to elevate their game to a new level of performance.

To prepare for the ensuing healthcare changes on the horizon, organizations need to change at a fundamental level. Creating sustainable systems that control expenses is only viable in facilities with the right infrastructure for support. Going from good to great starts with several key changes in the fabric of your culture that include

■ *Developing leadership alignment*: Aligning leadership toward a common goal to support the initiative and mobilize the organization.
■ *Creating a robust PI program*: Understanding past failures to design systems based on the latest PI methodologies.
■ *Restructuring your Project Management Office*: Creating a project tracking system that is poised for communication and accountability.
■ *Infrastructure and governance development*: Designing systems that maintain and grow themselves in a continuous quality improvement process. This effort is large in scale and mobilizes the organization toward a single cause.

Once the fundamentals are in place, the organization should be ready to pursue the primary opportunities across the enterprise for expense reduction and revenue enhancement. Examining the cost structure of most healthcare organizations reveals that more than 50% of operational expenses are in labor. This includes salaries, premium pay, benefits, bonuses, entitlements, and so on. The remaining costs are predominately divided between purchasing services, contracts, and supplies. These are the major categories that comprise the expense side of the equation.

Opportunities on the other side of the equation to enhance margins include access and revenue cycle optimization. Access is described as enhancing the ability of patients to get into the system using a smooth and timely process. This includes access to primary and specialty care providers, in addition to acute and post-acute care services. Closely related is revenue cycle enhancement, which includes making sure that processes are robust in collecting on every opportunity that is appropriate.

Modern methods of expense reduction think of traditional expenses as the symptoms of a greater disease that is inherent in the clinical treatment of the patient. This is predicated on the knowledge that approximately 80% of all healthcare costs are controlled by the provider. In this model, opportunities are inherent in clinical utilization and the treatment of patients as the basis of expense reduction. This leads to projects such as LOS, which targets the utilization of healthcare resources. These initiatives by default result in better labor management and lower supply costs, while providing better quality and service for the patient.

Although there are hundreds of other expense reduction opportunities within any organization, common strategies to reduce expenses and enhance revenue are typically categorized as follows:

- *Non-labor*: This is considered to be the biggest opportunity outside of labor for expense reductions. This includes opportunities such as utilization of supplies, testing, information management (IM), medical waste, and consolidation of products for economies of scale.
- *Labor*: This is considered to be the quickest expense reduction opportunity within most organizations. Opportunities for reductions in labor expenses include span of control restructuring, labor standards optimization, benefits management, and premium pay control.
- *LOS*: By controlling the LOS, other expense reduction strategies are enhanced immediately. This is considered a very progressive method of expense reduction that relies heavily on provider partnerships.

■ *Contracts*: This is the reduction of expenses without touching any FTEs. Contrary to popular belief, there are always opportunities to improve contract terms. With thousands of vendors contracted by a typical facility, this is often the easiest opportunity to pursue.

■ *Access*: This is considered to be the most basic of all opportunities to improve margins. These types of initiative work hard to remove every barrier between the patients and healthcare services.

■ *Revenue Enhancement*: This involves creating processes that collect every dollar owed—nothing more and nothing less. This includes management of both front office and back office functions.

The US healthcare system is set to account for more than 18% of our gross national product by the year 2020. With increasing demand for healthcare services, many providers are finding themselves caught in the perfect storm of regulatory, consumer, market, and reimbursement pressures. Consumers of healthcare, along with payors and providers, are all looking for value. This value proposition is redefining the priorities in many healthcare institutions.

Without a doubt, top performing organizations will build on our understanding of past failures to develop infrastructure and focus on initiatives that produce the most value for the patients and the organization. This book will define the steps required to develop infrastructure and finally design programs around major initiatives that have traditionally produced the highest returns. If you are already familiar with leadership alignment strategies and the power of a robust PI program, skip ahead to Chapter 5.

Chapter 2

Developing True Leadership Alignment

It's not enough to be busy, so are the ants. The question is, what are we busy doing?

Henry David Thoreau

Great strategies with unaligned initiatives will never go anywhere, and initiatives without support from leadership will result in nothing but frustration. The most important factor in making sure that all aspects of project execution fall into place is strong leadership alignment. This ensures that initiatives being implemented are aligned with the vision and mission of the organization, and garner support to remove barriers for success.

Organizational alignment starts at the top. In this regard, it is critical that leaders are fully aligned with a shared set of values, have a common purpose, and are capable of managing the key competencies that are required to meet the demands associated with strategies and internal/external conditions. Organizational and program leaders must demonstrate alignment and commitment to the vision, purpose, goals, and desired outcomes of the initiative. With misaligned strategies and priorities, initiatives are doomed to fail with unaffordable costs that can force many organizations into bankruptcy.

The vast majority of large-scale projects fail because of funding and management support. The costs associated with this failure rate are staggering. These costs typically fall into three buckets:

- *Financial capital*: Capital for investment is not easy to get in healthcare. With margins that are often less than 2%, many healthcare organizations find themselves falling further and further behind in technology, maintenance, and growth. With limited precious capital, any failure could have catastrophic effects on the financial viability of the organization.
- *Human capital*: Experts that have the skill set and experience to manage large-scale projects are limited and charge accordingly. Every failed project represents thousands of hours of manpower that would have been wasted. Additionally, failed projects demoralize project team members and stakeholders.
- *Time*: Time is money and for every day a project is not "live," the benefits are not being realized. For example, a project with a return of $40 million has an impact of about $100,000 a day. Healthcare is changing at such a fast pace that organizations that are slow to adapt can quickly find themselves in financial trouble.

There are many other costs, such as opportunity cost, frustration, retention, and so on, that are much harder to identify and quantify. In the end, every organization needs to understand the full cost of failure and create an environment and infrastructure to help the success of every initiative.

To avoid these costs, it is critical that organizations have a firm alignment between leadership, vision, mission, strategy, and initiatives. This linkage is the driver that produces the greatest outcomes in high-performing organizations. The strength of the alignment is based on the understanding and commitment of leadership to the process. This process in essence drives itself. In this model, each stage of the process depends on the previous one. Hence, there is an inherent connection both forward and backward in the process. Once this process breaks down at any point, the link is broken and misalignment occurs. See Exhibit 2.1.

At the heart of leadership alignment is making sure that the executive leaders are united behind the vision and mission of the organization. This step ensures that the strategies required for survival are understood and supported. The vision and mission need to be communicated with clarity to associates on a regular basis. This process ensures that the employees understand the direction of the business and the "why" behind the vision.

The next step is to identify and link the critical gaps between the current state and the future vision. These critical gaps are the basis of strategies that leadership develops to advance the organization. Once the strategies are formed, they are converted into initiatives. Strategies in and of themselves do not produce change. This is the critical step that is required to link the strategy to the envisioned outcomes. In

Exhibit 2.1   The five-phase alignment model linkage.

this process, there is a requirement for a constant review of the vision, gap, strategy, and initiatives to ensure alignment.

There are several key strategies that can be used to strengthen leadership alignment to large-scale initiatives. These include

1. Starting with the right leader
2. Clarity of vision
3. Practical communication of link between the mission, strategy and initiatives
4. Communicating obsessively
5. Involving senior executives in the initiatives
6. Strengthening the bond between Performance Improvement (PI) and the C-Suite

It goes without saying that creating a culture that promotes strong alignment between vision and strategy starts with the right leader. Making sure that the leaders are a good fit in the culture that created the vision is critical. Any misaligned priorities or objectives in the direction that the organization is going can derail multimillion dollar projects. Additionally, it can create confusion among the team members about priorities.

Clarity and simplicity in the vision, mission, and strategy of the organization is important to provide a clear path for associates to follow. Vision statements often become so complex that they are hard to remember or understand. Starting with an easy to follow vision and mission statement that is easy to remember is the key. I used to say that *Star Trek* had the best mission statement: "To boldly go where no man has gone before." In less than 10 words, they not only communicated what they were going to do, but how. Not only are they going to go where no man has gone before, but they are going to do it boldly.

Clarity often starts to break down as the vision and mission are converted into strategies and strategies into initiatives. The "why" is critical to garner support from the mid-level managers and frontline associates. If employees can't understand why they are doing what they are doing, then the project quickly loses its momentum and the passion behind the work goes away. It should be easy for anyone within the organization to see how his/her part in helping with a particular initiative will help themselves and the organization.

Linking the strategies to the initiatives has to be practical. For example, a vision might be to control the healthcare market in the South Florida region. This vision might require a strategy that takes control of the primary care provider networks. An initiative might be to buy up 100 practices annually to lock up the market. Here it is easy to see how every part is connected. It is in this simplicity and clarity that projects flourish and associates feel empowered.

Once the linkage is created, it is critical to communicate it to the associates. This requires more than a vision statement that we typically put on the hospital walls and elevators. The most critical part of this step is that leaders round with their staff and constituents to explain why they are doing what they do and the logic behind the strategy. This should be done as often as possible in open forums. Project managers (PMs) for large initiatives should certainly appreciate this, as they can make sure that what they are doing is a priority and continues to have the support of leadership.

Involving senior executives in major initiatives is critical. Good PMs typically identify project sponsors at the leadership level to provide guidance and support. Unfortunately, most PMs are still learning how to utilize sponsors effectively. Not communicating with, escalating issues to, or providing clarity in the roles of sponsors is a waste of time and money. Get the sponsors involved from the get-go during the planning phase. Bring them into meetings and provide constant updates. This includes information about benefits realization post go-live. This model of a hands-on approach with the sponsors is the best way to confirm and show support for the initiative.

The final key strategy is strengthening the alignment between the C-Suite and the PI leadership. Increasingly, in many organizations, the PI function is leading the charge for major strategic initiatives in lieu of the traditional functional leaders. The strength in the PI model is that projects often require multiple skill sets and an understanding of key disciplines for success. Typical PI expertise include assessments, implementations, program development, project tracking, and benefits realization, along with the traditional engineering functions such as analytics, Six Sigma, Lean, process measurements, and workflow review. These skills provide a strong foundation of project support for any initiatives that we typically see in healthcare. This puts the PI function in a very strong position to work closely with leadership to produce outcomes that drive strategy and in turn drive the mission.

The most advanced leadership alignment models between PI and the C-Suite in the industry consist of three key partnerships. These three partnerships make all the difference between good and great organizations. These include

- PI and the chief operating officer (COO)/chief executive officer (CEO) relationship
- PI and the chief financial officer (CFO) relationship
- PI and the vice president (VP) relationship

In order for large-scale strategic initiatives to have the best chance of success, there has to be a strong alignment within the senior leadership ranks. In the elevated PI model, the PI leader works closely with the CFO and the CEO/COO at a strategic level. Additionally, the PI leader works closely with the VP level leaders to remove barriers and drive projects at a tactical level. This relationship elevates the PI leader from a traditional tactical level to both a strategic and tactical level.

In this model, the CEO and the COO work closely with PI to identify and evaluate gaps in the current state and monitor organizational challenges. Together they strategize with finance to fully evaluate the impact. The CFO quantifies the impact of those changes to determine a financial or operational target. The opportunity is often broken down by impact over fiscal years and per month to see the opportunity cost. The PI function then leads the group in developing initiatives that financially and operationally close the gap to those targets. Once the initiatives are kicked off, the CFO and the CEO help support the PI initiatives to drive the organization forward. See Exhibit 2.2.

Case Study: In 2011, a 10-hospital system in Ohio was unable to negotiate favorable managed care rates. Because growth opportunities were limited in that market, the leadership decided to strategically focus on expense reduction strategies. The CFO developed a financial target that quantified the impact of these changes at $16 million for the next 3 years. The PI function brought the management team together and developed cost reduction initiatives to close the gap. In the meeting with senior leadership, the CEO explained the situation, the CFO quantified the situation, and the PI leader

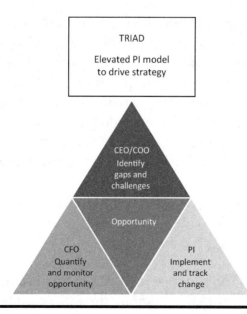

Exhibit 2.2   The elevated Performance Improvement triad model.

explained the opportunities and programs that would help them close the gaps. Once the program infrastructure was in place, the triad pushed the VP group to stay on schedule and within budget to achieve outcomes.

Alignment with the VP level leaders is the backbone that drives project execution. Although the triad is the head, the body of the work is done at the functional VP level. The VPs drive change and provide leadership for the associates. In 9 out of 10 cases when a project is falling behind, it is because team members do not have a clear vision and guidance from their function leader about their priorities. Making sure that the functional VPs create the linkage between the gap, the strategy, the target, and the initiatives is key. That same message has to be relayed to the team members and mid-level leaders.

At a strategic level, leaders typically manage large-scale problems. And large-scale problems require large-scale solutions. By default, this requires help from every functional area. Every VP has to be aligned and in support of the direction that the organization is headed in.

Leveraging the CFO and the CEO to realign the VPs priorities is important because there are always competing programs and requirements that will come up. The definition of realignment by senior leadership is important because most organizations don't know the difference between support and commitment. In a recent presentation, a speaker discussed how the chicken providing the egg for breakfast was supportive of a good breakfast. But the pig representing bacon was committed. This is the intensity that needs to be driven through the triad to the functional leaders. The triad cannot have any reservations about interacting with colleagues to hold them accountable.

Making sure that there is alignment between the initiative team members and the functional VPs is important. There are several key drivers that strengthen the functional teams to produce great outcomes. These include a clear understanding of

- Team expectations
- Team commitment
- Personalizing the mission
- Providing support

Defining team expectations at the beginning of any initiative is critical to preventing any confusion. No different from linking the expectations of senior leadership to the functional VPs, this same process needs to occur with the team members. This step creates accountability within the group in front of the functional VPs so there are no misunderstandings. This includes a full review of deliverables, dates, and commitments to outcomes.

Team commitment is part of the dynamic that keeps the project moving forward when resources are tight. It is important that the senior leadership show their commitment to the project so that the team members can use that to set expectations. A few tricks of the trade include engaging the team members prior to kick-off to get their buy-in. Additionally, if team members have a say in how the plan is created, they will have an inherent commitment to the initiative. The opposite of nurturing commitment is creating plans and strategies that are created independent of those doing the work and attaching unrealistic and unfeasible constraints.

By personalizing the initiatives, one can create an environment that directly connects the team member to the vision and mission of the organization. This strategy creates a link between the vision and the tasks being performed at the project level. Most people who enter the healthcare field do so because they want to help others. The ability to show how the vision and mission are aligned with the project tasks can further that cause. In essence, team members can support themselves by supporting the organizational objectives and projects.

In the 2009 book *The Army of Alexander the Great* by Stephen English, it was explained that Alexander the Great conquered Greece by the age of 22. His hallmark for leadership was based on his bravery in going to the frontlines in support of his soldiers. This was the most significant differentiator that made him great in the eyes of many military historians. Leadership commitment to supporting the frontline team members is a key strategy for setting expectations, showing commitment, and providing support. The PI leader can provide much of this support in the form of engineering tools such as workflow analysis, statistical process reviews, and reporting.

In order to keep organizations on top, leadership alignment is critical. This includes linking the vision to the mission, the gap requirements, the strategies, the initiatives, and ultimately the outcomes. A key strategy in accomplishing this is to create an elevated PI model that utilizes a triad of the CEO/COO, CFO, and PI leader to create an engine that produces a strong linkage at the top. This linkage is extended to the functional VPs and ultimately to the project team members, thereby completing the alignment loop.

Chapter 3

Creating a Robust Performance Improvement Program

> Insanity is doing the same thing over and over again and expecting different results.
>
> **Albert Einstein**

In a recent healthcare conference, I was asked what it takes to develop the optimal Performance Improvement (PI) program. My response was, "Twenty-five years of having done it the wrong way." With decreasing margins, many organizations have turned to PI to help navigate the never-ending cycle of improving margins, quality, and service. With mixed outcomes, it is challenging for leaders to develop a robust PI function that can deliver big results.

The healthcare industry is currently experiencing change at an unprecedented rate. These changes started more than 30 years ago when we realized that there are not enough resources to support the double-digit growth rates in expenses and demand for services. The impacts of government regulations, reductions in reimbursements, market pressures, and consumerism have led healthcare organizations into a frenzy as they fight for their survival.

PI functions have been used for several decades in healthcare with mixed results. These mixed results have created a sawtooth effect that sees an endless cycle of program downsizing and redeployment. Many organizations see PI functions as something nice to have, but not a requirement. This failure in understanding the function at its core level is due primarily to the inability of PI leaders to show the value of their functions. For this reason, many consulting companies are often engaged in tough economic times to deliver fast and measurable results, completely bypassing PI programs.

There are several underlying reasons for the past failure of many PI programs to deliver on promised results. They include methodology, speed, leadership support, tracking, and coordination. It is critical to analyze and understand these failures of the past in order to transform systems and processes to deliver on future expectations.

Modern day healthcare PI methodologies have their roots in manufacturing. The greatest accomplishments occurred during the Industrial Revolution with the major wars as catalysts. Modern methodologies started in the 1970s and 1980s with total quality management (TQM) and continuous quality improvement (CQI) processes. These methods were the foundation of future programs such as Six Sigma and Lean Thinking that we see today.

Sigma, σ, is a letter in the Greek alphabet used by statisticians to measure the variability in any process. Defects are measured in parts per million with Six Sigma being the target representing just 3.4 defects per million. It is based on the DMAIC process that requires initiatives to go through a very disciplined methodology by defining the problem, measuring it, analyzing it, improving it, and finally making any required controls for guidance. See Exhibit 3.1.

Six Sigma had its origins in Motorola and expanded its capability at GE. The value of Six Sigma over previous

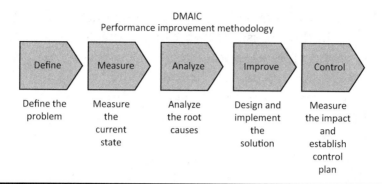

DMAIC
Performance improvement methodology

Define	Measure	Analyze	Improve	Control
Define the problem	Measure the current state	Analyze the root causes	Design and implement the solution	Measure the impact and establish control plan

Exhibit 3.1   The DMAIC methodology process.

programs such as TQM and CQI was that it required management participation. Through the Black Belt and Green Belt governance, projects were required to have sponsors and managers. This was an important distinction in that management buy-in and involvement was recognized as part of any strong PI program. It is estimated that most of the Fortune 500 companies today have a Six Sigma program.

Lean Thinking is another powerful methodology that has taken healthcare by storm. The fundamental notion behind this methodology is to maximize customer value while minimizing waste. Basically, Lean Thinking means doing more with less, thereby creating more value for customers with fewer resources.

Lean organizations strive to have a strong understanding of customer value and focus resources to continuously improve these processes relentlessly. The final goal in Lean Thinking is to provide perfect value to the customer through a perfect value creation process that has zero waste. This means nothing more and nothing less than what the customer expects.

In order to maximize value, Lean Thinking changes the focus of management from optimizing separate technologies, assets, and vertical departments to optimizing the flow of products and services through entire value streams that flow horizontally across technologies, assets, and departments to customers.

The reason why many of these methodologies have not worked in healthcare is that they can be complex, resource intensive, and prolonged. In the early 2000s, Six Sigma programs were growing rapidly throughout the healthcare industry. Many organizations paid as much as $10,000 per person training leaders in the methodology, hoping that it would provide innovative solutions for their facilities. Through train-the-trainer programs, this methodology was disseminated to mid-level managers overnight. Today, almost everyone in healthcare is familiar with Lean and Six Sigma terms if not the methodologies.

Part of the failure of these methodologies was inherent in its complexity. The vast majority of healthcare employees rose through the ranks as clinicians. As clinicians, they have very little training in statistics, analytics, project management, and process engineering. Calculating the Six Sigma levels in their daily processes was difficult, burdensome, and hard to understand. Hence, many trained Black Belts stopped using the methodology and have instead opted for a more practical version for PI.

Another major flaw in this methodology was the speed at which projects came to fruition. Understanding workflow and processes, measuring each function, analyzing for variation, creating actions plans, and finally implementing changes takes time. In some cases, it can take 6 months or more. With the fast pace of change in healthcare, by the time many of these programs are in the implementation phase, the original processes and protocols have already changed.

Increasingly, CEOs see time as a luxury that no longer exists in healthcare at the current rate of change. This inability to bring projects to fruition quickly was a major obstacle in showing value for PI initiatives. Many consulting companies filled this void by developing rapid implementation cycle programs. In a matter of weeks, consultants would utilize benchmarking data, query the staff for improvement ideas, and go into implementation mode within 120 days. This left many organizations rethinking strategic PI as a viable function within their facilities with enough value to sustain its life.

Another major failure of past PI programs has been the inability of program managers to garner leadership support. This is due to several factors including the reporting relationship, misunderstanding of the function, and promotion of unquantifiable projects. Traditionally, many PI leaders have felt comfortable with process mapping, throughput engineering, and opportunity studies. These initiatives are hard to quantify as they often have no direct impact on revenue or expenses. In many opportunity studies, although the opportunity is quantified, the implementation is often handed down to the operators, which introduces risk to the completion of the project. Without a return on interest (ROI) for every project, the risk of not being able to justify the function grows over time.

By and large, the most important failure of the PI function is based on its inability to provide robust project management skills that promote the execution of plans. Traditionally, PI programs have been excellent at measuring, process mapping, and calculating the opportunities. The inability to convert the opportunity into actionable steps and hold management accountable has been at the crux of why most organizations fail in executing great plans.

Under this assumption, implementation becomes the key aspect of any great program that strives to take an organization from good to great. To define this further, in order to make change and provide true process transformation within any organization, there needs to be targets, clarity, accountability, and teamwork.

To create an environment that supports strong leadership alignment, project execution, accountability, and a focus on results, the culture has to change. By developing strong processes and infrastructure around these tactics, process transformation will begin to take shape. Many top performing organizations create this new culture by designing and developing a robust PI program.

As the current healthcare delivery model prepares to undergo the next generation of changes, these are the top 10 strategies that can keep your PI program poised to deliver results.

While change is nothing new to healthcare, the rate at which this change will occur is going to accelerate. CMS is leading the charge with most payors lined up behind them on the march to control costs by reducing reimbursements. With the advent of bundled payments, VBP, MSPB, ACO, MSSP, and HEDIS, pay-for-performance strategies are only going to grow from here. The industry is resigned to the fact that many of us will not survive this transition as the strong get stronger and the weak become consolidated.

All these changes mean only one thing to the healthcare industry: do more with less. To prepare for the next generation of changes, it is imperative that every organization design and develop a PI program that can begin preparing the organization for this reality ahead of the competition. Here are the top 10 strategies every high-performing PI department should be considering in the coming decade:

1. *Bring in the right PI leadership that can envision big results*: Historically, many PI programs typically worked on departmental level projects that often produce results that are hard to quantify. It's true that incremental change can add up, but healthcare is changing at a rapid pace and our ability to produce large-scale results is critical. In practical terms, a 1% reduction in expenses across the system year after year should be par for the course, regardless of the organization's ability to meet the budget. The right PI leader will have the vision, knowledge, and influence to develop the right infrastructure and mobilize the organization for this type of continuous transformation.

   The growth of consulting companies in recent years is a testament to the fact that most PI departments have been struggling to change at the same rate as the current healthcare environment. The right PI leader will develop a good balance between the science behind process engineering and the discipline of consulting companies to implement large-scale changes.

It is critical to understand that these senior PI leaders are not your typical PI managers coming through the ranks. They are motivated by large-scale change in performance across the enterprise, operating very similar to a quasi-system-level chief operations officer (COO) function.

2. *PI leaders of the future have to work closely with system-level COOs and chief financial officers (CFOs) to produce results*: With large-scale changes come large-scale problems. Without the support of the leaders that control these functions across the system, it's hard to make any changes. This is exacerbated in healthcare because of the silos inherent in the current delivery models. With the proper systems, the CFO can help identify the burning platform and develop targets. The PI function can mobilize the organization and identify the projects to achieve those goals. The COO can help remove barriers to get results. All three have to work in concert for large-scale change to occur.

In many organizations, there is a false expectation that the PI program, through training the organization in Lean, Six Sigma, and data analysis, will produce millions in savings. Without the right support behind every PI initiative, it is nearly impossible to mobilize the resources and remove the barriers required for success.

3. *Keep your PI department lean*: Good PI programs often become victims of their own success. As the benefits start rolling in, it is hard not to grow the function so long as the ROI is there. Unfortunately, at some point when there is a downturn, overgrown, non-revenue generating

functions are the first targets for cost reduction strategies. To keep this problem in check, always target an eight-to-one return on projects. Traditional throughput or full-time equivalent (FTE) analysis projects that assist at the departmental level are good at helping struggling managers but should be balanced with large-scale projects that span the enterprise.

A good rule of thumb is to staff the PI department with one FTE for every $200 million in net revenue the organization makes. This includes engineers, analysts, and project managers (PMs) combined. This number may seem high, but start by taking inventory of your personnel. By the time you add up the decision support functions, PMs, departmental analysts, quality improvement analysts, and process engineers, it will be interesting to see where you sit.

4. *Create a permanent organizational governance structure for PI initiatives*: It's critical that healthcare organizations understand clearly that the PI function lives in a world that will never stop looking for opportunities. The idea behind improving margins, service, and quality will continue to persist in the next decade as it has for the last 20+ years. Begin by taking stock of what infrastructure is in place to implement change. Are the right steering committees, working groups, task teams, tracking mechanisms, and personnel in place? Does everyone understand their responsibility, reporting matrices, report-outs, and escalation processes?

Categorize projects into major initiatives, that is, non-labor, labor, and so on. Each initiative needs to have its own steering committee, working groups, and teams. A good strategy is to assign a steering committee member to each project lead as their go-to person to help remove barriers. The working groups are the go-getters. They don't wait until the next steering committee meeting to get the teams moving. In the middle of all this activity, your PI staff should be supporting each team, working group members, and steering committee leaders. Without this infrastructure to support your objectives, your initiatives will be dead on arrival.

5. *Redefine your Project Management Office (PMO) project life cycle*: In the next decade, our definition of the project life cycle will have to change to maximize the value that the PMO brings to organizations. Today, most PMO directors typically find themselves clipping and pasting monthly updates from PMs into a master file and then distributing this to leadership. Some advanced programs provide resourcing and Gantt charts about the status of the projects. In essence, the life cycle starts after the approval of the project and is complete at the point when the operators signed off at go-live. The value that this PMO model provides to leadership is minimal compared to what it can do.

   To optimize your PI function, it is imperative to have a PMO function that operates at a whole new level. This means that we have to understand the "why" behind the "what." By expanding the project life cycle definition to include project procurement and benefits realization, the entire function of the PMO changes. Ultimately, we have forgotten that these projects are all related to some effect or result that we are looking to achieve. Whether it's an electronic medical record system, a new emergency center, or a quality initiative, we are looking for results. The project is not over unless the intended outcomes have been measured and achieved. Future PMO functions need to include project procurement and justification on the front end and benefits realization on the back end in all their tracking. Always remember that activity in itself is not a substitute for results.

Additionally, it is critical that the PMO tracks both project indicators and organizational metrics that the project was planned to impact. These are what we typically call *leading* and *lagging indicators*. This differentiation is critical because a project can be 100 percent on target but may not have impacted your organizational metrics or vice versa.

6. *Focus on 90-day projects that maximize your returns*: Just a few months after my certification as a Six Sigma Master Black Belt, I quickly set out to conquer patient throughput. The project was very intensive and required significant amounts of measurements and calculations. It took almost 6 months to capture all the right data sets and identify potential solutions. By the time I was ready to move forward with implementation, many of the original measurements were obsolete, along with many of the solutions. This was an important lesson as healthcare processes and regulations are changing so fast that projects which go beyond 90 to 120 days are at risk of becoming obsolete. It's difficult to avoid large-scale projects, so a good strategy might be to break the initiative down into 120-day projects. For example, non-labor is a perpetual CQI process but it may be made up of over a hundred individual projects that span 90 to 120 days each.

    Stay away from initiatives that have less than $1 million in returns. There is a distinction that needs to be made here in that individual projects and tasks may have limited opportunity, but the initiative as a whole should be over $1 million. For example, our target for non-labor this year is in the millions and is made of 189 projects.

7. *Make complex information easy to understand and actionable*: Data presentation is key in order to help managers and leaders stay aligned and focused. Your graph has to tell a story that is compelling and easy to

understand. Here are five tips to help you have a big impact:

1. Start by thinking about what it is you want to communicate with leadership. For example, it's not just length of stay that you want to show, but maybe the mismanagement of the outliers. It's critical to continually think about the message as you look through your opportunities.

2. Make the graphs actionable. Help leaders and staff focus on what the graph is trying to say. In explaining the information, you can help them take the next step toward their solution. For example, we show monthly Hospital Consumer Assessment of Healthcare Providers and Systems (HCAHPS) scores to the staff and leaders. It was not until leadership saw the impact of three units on the entire system that the information became very actionable. PI departments have to learn to use existing tools more effectively in order to mobilize the organization.

3. Use the right graph for the right purpose. Don't use a bar graph to show trends. Scatter plots are not good for showing expenses and revenues. There is a one-page cheat sheet that the American Society for Quality (ASQ) uses for their SSBB certifications, which I still refer to even after 25 years.

4. Help your viewer to focus on information in the graph that tells the story. For example, in a table, show highlighted sections that you want the viewer to focus on. Often, it's hard to find the perfect graph that has the impact you may be looking for. A trick is to slice and dice it in as many different ways as possible, until the picture you hope to show begins to appear.

5. Healthcare is very complex and it's important to present information clearly in order to help leaders connect the dots. For example, I shared retention data by leader in one graph, then I showed service scores by leader and finally the correlation between the two. The

correlation showed clearly that it's the same managers that typically have low scores in both categories. Most leaders know this intuitively but you can help bring the science to it.

8. *PI departments need a new breed of staff that can manage the entire project life cycle*: For many years, PI departments were in the business of doing benchmarking, workflows, and time studies to show opportunities. These opportunities would often go to finance for quantification and if approved would be turned over to the operators for implementation. Unfortunately, healthcare is still designed as silos and it's difficult to make sure that all projects make it from conception to benefits realization in this process.

   To counter this problem, PI engineers need to have the ability to cut across all these disciplines. The ultimate PI staff will have their traditional PI training, but will also have financial training to quantify the opportunity, and project management skills to implement the solution if required. This will give the PI department the skill set to control a project from identification to benefits realizations.

   When evaluating a candidate's resume, there are a whole host of terms that we typically scan for, such as process engineering, Lean, and Six Sigma. But more valuable candidates will also have terms such as finance, MBA, project management, and PMP certification. The future of PI does not differentiate between process engineering, finance, and project management. Each staff member will have to manage the initiative through the entire project life cycle.

9. *If you are going to do Lean Six Sigma training across the enterprise, do it in a meaningful way*: Many healthcare organizations today have put their hat on the latest

PI methodologies to improve operations. With or without help from consulting companies in implementing these tools, organizations have had mixed results. Lean Six Sigma in itself can be a very powerful tool, if implemented correctly. Learning Japanese or shuffling everyone through class has been an absolute failure in most organizations. We have to remember that most mid-level managers and directors using these tools to improve operations have come through the ranks based on their mastery of clinical knowledge. The sooner we come to terms with this, the sooner we will be able to leverage Lean and Six Sigma in a way that can actually have an impact.

In the next decade, organizations that structure the Lean programs around small personalized classes with expectations from mandatory projects will reap the biggest rewards. In this structure, each student is required to come up with a project that has to be completed before certification is given. These projects have to be quantifiable to the tune of $25,000–$50,000 in annual savings. In this model, the expectations are set before the class even starts. It is critical that the PI department help the Lean Six Sigma students in the initial stages to kick-start projects through brainstorming, workflow, and analytics. This can be done by assigning each student a PI engineer as the go-to person to kick-start the projects when the class is over. To keep the initiatives moving, the PMO needs to bring these PMs back monthly for review and updates on their projects.

10. *Good PI programs will need to leverage information and innovations across the enterprise*: As the number of consolidations increase in healthcare, the number of opportunities is also increasing. The ability to leverage innovations and solutions from isolated departments across the enterprise can help improve quality and service, and reduce costs without much effort.

The eighth source of waste in Lean is our inability to leverage the minds of the people who work in our organizations. We typically pay staff to complete their tasks and, even though they are the experts, we rarely go to them for advice on improving the process. There is a reason why step one of most consulting engagements is the employee interviews. Conceptually, employee suggestion programs can help leverage this untapped potential. If done right, it can produce a significant ROI.

It's true that we have been working on the same problems for over 20 years, but healthcare is complex and we have to constantly look for innovations that we did not think of before. Organizations such as the Health Information Management Systems Society (HIMSS) and the Society of Health Systems (SHS) are great resources for sharing innovations. For benchmarking, organizations such as Truven, TBS, and Premier have a plethora of resources available to share best practices. The best PI programs are always looking for opportunities to be on the cutting edge of innovation.

Many existing PI programs have been unable to compete with consulting companies in providing large-scale changes that impact the bottom line quickly. This is evidenced by the fact that many of these internal programs are downsized when margins run into the red. Theoretically, it is for this very moment that PI functions have been built. The fact that leadership often decides to downsize this function is a testament to the failure of PI programs to provide value for their organizations.

By making a few fundamental changes in how PI departments function, it's possible to convert the existing PI program into high-functioning internal consulting units that are no different to the services that external consulting companies provide. With these 10 PI strategies, you can develop a robust internal PI program that can produce large-scale results at a fraction of the cost of external consultants.

Chapter 4

Upgrade the Project Management Office

> However beautiful the strategy, you should occasionally look at the results.

> **Winston S. Churchill**

Healthcare companies have experienced dramatic cuts in reimbursements over the last three decades. These changes have put a significant burden on organizations to change and create new delivery models that do more with less. The engine that drives this transformation includes the projects, initiatives, and programs that incrementally change day-to-day activities by restructuring and redefining people, processes, and technology. This in turn changes the culture and delivery models of the organization slowly over time.

Unfortunately, project management has not had a great reputation for success in the healthcare industry. The Gartner Group releases statistics annually that show the abysmal rates of project failure across various industries. This failure to deliver on expectations has resulted in losses that are calculated in the billions. With precious resources and low margins, many healthcare organizations have turned to the Project Management Office (PMO) as the solution to reducing losses.

Controlled project management begins at the portfolio level, where the strategic vision drives initial investments and where value is measured. A fully aligned project, program, and portfolio management strategy encompasses the entire organization, dictating project execution at every level and aiming to deliver value at each step along the way. Project management is, in fact, shorthand for project, program, and portfolio management. Increasingly, healthcare organizations are clearly seeing the payoff from investing time, money, and resources into building organizational project management expertise. The benefits include lower costs, greater efficiencies, improved quality and customer satisfaction, and a greater competitive advantage.

With tight margins, every dollar counts in healthcare and increasing the success rate of initiatives by just 10 can represent millions to the bottom line. To manage projects at a higher level of performance, healthcare organizations need to adapt and learn to invest in new PMO deployment models. The value of an upgraded PMO function that understands the importance of an expanded definition of the project life cycle, and the required future skills of project managers (PMs), is critical to great project execution. Although there are many project management models being used today that are specialized by industry, healthcare typically uses the centralized and decentralized model.

The centralized model has full control over the resourcing of initiatives. In this model, all PMs and project coordinators report to the PMO and are resourced to the projects as they are approved. Typically, projects are tracked in the PMO system and updates are provided to stakeholders and leadership on a routine basis with a disciplined project management methodology.

The decentralized model, also known as the subscription model, provides project management consulting services to functional areas that have been given funding and approval to move forward with initiatives. In this model, the utilization of services is optional and PMs can be existing operators. There is no standard project management methodology and no set tools. Each project is in essence customized to fit what is required for the success of that project by the stakeholder.

Both models have a very strict definition of a project or initiative. In this definition, a project is temporary in nature in that it has a defined beginning and end date, and therefore a defined scope and resources. The project is also unique in that it is not a routine operation, but a specific set of operations designed to accomplish a singular goal. The project team often includes people from multiple disciplines. The development of a new electronic medical record (EMR), labor management system, or length of stay process re-engineering initiative are all considered new projects, and must be managed effectively to deliver the results that organizations are pursuing. Project management can ultimately be defined as the application of knowledge, skills, tools, and techniques to project activities to meet the project objectives that drive the organizational vision.

Over time, the project management methodologies have developed five key processes that define the existing project life cycle from kick-off to go-live. These include

- Initiating
- Planning
- Executing
- Monitoring and controlling
- Closing

The first phase of the project management process is initiating. In this step, the team assesses the project objectives and desired outcome. Project deliverables, measures of success, and outcomes are defined in detail and documented. Additionally, at this stage, the team develops the scheduling and budgeting of the project. This is a critical step as almost all projects are measured by two key indicators: being on budget and being on time. Setting the right expectations of time and money up-front are key to having a successful outcome.

Planning is the second phase of the process and involves creating plans to help guide the project through the execution and closure phases. The plans created during this phase will assist the team and stakeholders in managing time, cost, quality, change, risk, and issues. At the same time, they will help PMs control team members to ensure delivery of the project on time and on budget.

The execution phase is the third phase of the project management process and is typically the most resource-intensive part of the project. During the execution phase, the project team develops the product or service and presents the final product to the customer for sign-off. The execution phase is the longest in duration because this is where transformation occurs. This is why it is the most resource-intensive phase of the project.

The monitoring and controlling phases of the project management process steer the initiative in the optimal direction to keep it on budget and on time. Project controls are the data gathering, management, and analytical processes used to predict, understand, and influence the time and cost outcomes of a project or program. The scope of monitoring and control encompasses quality controls, integration processes, documentation, and analytics.

The closing phase consists of the processes that are performed to officially finish and close all the assignments in a project or phase. The concluding action in this group will usually include the approval and transfer of the project deliverables to the user or customer. It is important that all actions that are included in the closing group are performed thoroughly, as only then will a project be considered closed. The essence of this group is that all the stakeholders agree that the project has met its assigned objectives. Furthermore, the staff and other resources can be reassigned to other projects, or relieved if not required.

Project management methodologies and models have come far in the last few decades. With the development of the Project Management Institute (PMI), the methodologies have become more consistent and mainstream. Additionally, with PMI certifications becoming ever more popular, a bar has been set that shows the ability of an individual to speak and understand the PM language.

Even with this development, the existing project management model still has its weaknesses. These weaknesses are evident in a recent industry report that indicated a 50% failure rate in healthcare projects. The foundation of this failure is almost always rooted in project support from senior leadership and benefit realization. As many technology developers say, it's almost never the technology.

The flaw in the existing project life cycle today is that it starts at the point of kick-off and ends at go-live. Although there is an initiating and planning phase in the existing model, it is predominately a function of a project that has already been approved and funded. There is little understanding of the outcomes that are desired and reasons behind the initiative. Additionally, in the existing model, the benefits are almost never calculated in the outcomes that were originally desired after go-live. The success of the project is measured by the ability of the PM to implement the system or the process.

For example, a multi-hospital system in Florida recently implemented an EMR for many reasons, one of which was to eliminate paper. The project started at the planning kick-off and ended at go-live 6 months later when the clinicians were using the system. Although the system was being used, the paper trail never went away. For various reasons, such as governmental agencies and patient signatures, paper was still around and now had to be scanned and put into the system. Although the project execution was a success, not all the originally identified benefits were realized. This was not discovered until a year later when margins were getting smaller as operational costs went up and leadership was asking for a review of the benefits that the investment in the EMR was supposed to bring.

In this case, the PM was never aware of all the reasons behind the approval of the project and, additionally, never went back to measure and see if all those assumptions were realized. Although the project was a success in the eyes of the PM, it was a failure in the eyes of leadership and those that originally approved the project. This situation occurs in about 50% of healthcare projects according to the Gartner Group. This represents billions in waste throughout the industry.

To counter this failure rate, many organizations have started to expand the definition of the project life cycle to include procurement before kick-off and benefits realization after go-live. With this change, the culture of the project management team changes to focus on outcomes and not just implementation of the project. In this new expanded model, the project is flanked on either end with procurement and benefits realization. See Exhibit 4.1.

Project procurement is the process by which a project is born. It includes four key functions that lead to kick-off:

- Strategy development
- Opportunity identification
- Feasibility
- Approval and funding

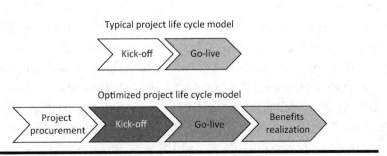

Exhibit 4.1   The expanded project life cycle model.

Many of the problems associated with project failures that result from the inability to realize the identified benefits start long before the project is approved and funded. The PMs need to understand and absorb the connection between their project and the end state that the leadership is trying to achieve. This includes being a part of strategy decisions, opportunity development, feasibility studies, and ultimately project approval.

For example, in an organization recently after the implementation of an EMR, it was determined that half the benefits that were expected from the rollout of a new system were not realized. Later it was discovered that the project team did not implement the dictation and transcription module based on some technical issues. They had no idea that almost half the system's return on investment was based on implementing this one module. Not making the connection between the project go-live and the expected outcomes is rooted in an existing project life cycle that does not require any understanding of what precipitated the project. It is critical that the project life cycle incorporates the project procurement process as a required step before project kick-off.

Just like project procurement, benefits realization after a project go-live is critical to a high-performing PMO function. Most leaders typically do not measure success once the project moves past go-live. It is almost always assumed that the benefits will automatically follow. This is a big assumption that is typically not true in healthcare projects, as evidenced by the current failure rates. It is not until months or often years later that leadership begins asking questions about projects that never materialized the benefits they were expecting. For this reason, no project is over until the benefits of the project have been tallied and the outcomes measured against the original expectations of leadership.

Forward-looking PMs that have significant experience working with top leadership are aligned with the business and operational expectations. This alignment is inherent in the daily tools they use to manage projects. Good PMs utilize tracking systems that typically monitor tasks, due dates, duration, predecessors, and those responsible for different elements. Great PMs use three additional columns to track progress in their project tracking tools:

1. Target opportunity
2. Benefits identified
3. Benefits realized

Target opportunity is a metric that represents the original opportunity projected by leadership prior to doing a full-blown assessment of the project. For example, in non-labor initiatives, benchmarking is often used to identify the target opportunity for prioritization. This number can vary substantially from what is actually identified or realized. It is a crude method of calculating an opportunity as a placeholder to get a rough idea of what can be expected.

Benefits identified is the calculated opportunity recognized by leadership once a detailed internal assessment is completed. The more detailed the assessment, the more confidence the team will have going into the project regarding what is expected. This number is very erratic in that it can land either above or below the originally identified target. Great PMs study the assessments in order to get a good handle on how benefits were identified and calculated. Any flaws or erroneous assumptions in the study can render the best PM frustrated at benefits realization.

Benefits realized is the portion of the identified benefits that were actually recognized as achieved and documented in the financials. This is the last phase of the project that confirms if the benefits were achieved and documented through data audits. Typically, this portion of the project is completed by the financial function to create an unbiased process. Benefits realized is critical to the project, as it represents the results to those who envisioned the change from the very beginning.

It is critical that this step of the process is always completed even if the sponsor of the project does not require it. Experience shows that it is almost inevitable that questions will come up even years later about major initiatives. In many organizations, as leadership changes, all major assumptions of the past are often reviewed. Every great PM should be ready to show the value of the projects in a definitive format.

The project tracking tools of the future will have to incorporate these metrics as just another part of managing a project or an initiative. These new PM tools increasingly hold the project accountable to its original purpose and expected outcomes. This is no different than the way the "task owners" are accountable for completing their tasks on time and on budget. It is for this reason that in many forward-thinking organizations, the project tracking tools are often called accountability tools.

Take the time and truly invest in understanding the business expectations and functionality of the project. Ensure that there is proof of concept with plenty of data to support the assumptions. Track carefully the financials at every step of the process from benefits identification to benefits realization. Allow for good processes for revisiting the expectations and required funding at multiple points during the project.

In review, as the project management life cycle is expanded to incorporate procurement and benefits realization, project success rates will inherently begin to rise. This expansion of the definition also requires a new breed of PMs with new skill sets to manage the project. This includes financial expertise for benefits realization and outcome calculations in addition to process engineering skills that help with opportunity identification and operational assessments.

In the project procurement phase, ideas are evaluated, measured, and assessed for opportunity. Great PMs start at this stage of the process and are fully vested in sitting side by side with operators as they design the future state operationally. To understand and contribute at this stage of the process, future PMs need to have basic knowledge of workflow assessment, activity measurement, and data analytics. As PMs incorporate this step into the process, all the assumptions and objectives become evident and this creates clarity in the transformation process.

In the benefits realization phase, PMs are required to speak with authority about the financial and operational objectives of the project. As all the outcomes can be quantified by some measure, it is critical that future PMs have a basic understanding of accounting and financial rules. This skill is critical in that, at the end of the project, it's all about the returns and outcomes. And if something cannot be measured, then it is not worth doing for most leaders.

With these simple changes in people, processes, and technology that form part of the PMO function, an organization can increase the chances of success significantly.

Running an upgraded PMO function requires a combination of both traditional and innovative tools. Traditional tools that are commonly used to run projects are project charters, agendas, minutes, and tracking forms. New innovative tools include project portfolio management systems, integrated communication systems, and modified tracking tools.

Project portfolio management systems have gained popularity in recent years for large-scale project management controls for larger facilities. Portfolio management refers to running multiple projects at a strategic level. In this perspective, project portfolio management is more than running multiple projects. Each portfolio of projects is required to be assessed on its business value and adherence to the strategy.

Powerful PMO software solutions such as Project Insight, Dapulse, and Clarizen have been developed to manage complex projects at the portfolio level. These systems control projects tightly and prevent common mistakes from occurring by designing customized processes that eliminate human error. These systems provide overall scheduling of resources, summary progress reports, and the impact of projects on each other. This is critical as project portfolios that consist of hundreds of projects are too difficult for the human brain to process and manage.

Some of the more sophisticated systems such as Clarizen provide integrated communication systems with PMs and task owners. This integrated approach allows for the system to automatically interact with project owners by requesting updates based on due dates and allows the task owners to update status updates remotely. The power of these systems lies in the project planning and setup. Once the project is input into the system, the software runs itself.

Project tracking tools vary but they need to be modified to accommodate the new models of delivery. Excel is always a popular tool for project tracking. New tracking tools need to include items such as financial measures, vice presidents assigned to specific team members, and barriers preventing progress. A sample of a modified tracking tool is provided at the end of this book as a model for a strong project-tracking process.

Changing the project life cycle model and upgrading infrastructure tools are essential for creating a robust PMO function within your organization. These infrastructure changes create the environment for project management optimization to occur. Although tools provide the basic foundation, it is the cultural transformation that drives the expectations in this new environment. The optimal project management culture is one where there is strong leadership accountability. Technology and tracking systems are used to help and hold each other accountable with rapid escalation processes. All team members are expected to attend the meetings or send a designate. Difficult questions are asked to remove difficult barriers quickly. Finally, efforts are made to ensure that the right person is on the team. See Exhibit 4.2.

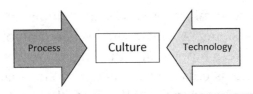

Exhibit 4.2 Processes and technology are the key enablers that allow management to hold each other accountable and begin changing the culture.

Leadership accountability is the key part of any high-performing PMO function. This includes making sure that leaders are driving the charge for change, assisting with removing barriers and resolving problems as soon as they are escalated. Additionally, leaders need to understand that if assigned team members are unable to perform their function, they need to resolve the situation. The leader has to remove all barriers so that team members can perform their duties.

For a strong execution of initiatives, a critical step in developing infrastructure is to develop a robust PMO function. This includes expanding the project life cycle, providing tools that help monitor and track returns on investment, and ultimately holding the leaders accountable. In this model of performance, an organization is almost guaranteed a better success rate than its competitors.

Chapter 5

Governance Structure: The Engine for Sustainability

It is not the beauty of a building you should look at;
it's the construction of the foundation that will stand
the test of time.

David Allan Coe

Although governance infrastructure has a variety of mean-
ings across the healthcare industry, in this book it is defined
broadly to include any part of a system in which guidance and
control is required to produce a desired outcome. The simplest
definition of governance is the framework for effective decision making and control for good execution. Additionally, it
provides a way for leadership to exercise effective oversight to
ensure strategies are appropriately implemented, prioritized,
and maintained. In this definition, project governance sits
outside of the project management domain and is applied to
perpetually functioning continuous quality improvement (CQI)
systems and programs.

The secret to my success in delivering bottom-line financial results year after year has always been in developing an A+ governance infrastructure. It took years to understand what this meant and to learn that there is more value in building a great system that never stops than trying to do it all yourself. In this model, the organization designs programs and systems that work smarter, not harder. Experienced Performance Improvement (PI) leaders tap into this power of true synergy not because they are lazy, but because it is *efficient* and *productive*. It is efficient in that it utilizes all the resources available for an initiative, and productive in that it can produce more value than any single person in a lifetime individually.

Finding the correct strategy in developing a robust governance infrastructure makes all the difference between organizations that can never find their way to results and those that see them every day. A common disappointment in the last two decades has been the sustainability of programs. Part of the solution is in building a great infrastructure that controls output. The basis of this model is rooted in the CQI concepts of the 1980s.

Certain initiatives such as labor and non-labor will never go away, so creating a system that can produce outcomes perpetually is critical. Designing systems with a robust governance infrastructure creates an environment that allows people, processes, and technology to work perpetually toward an objective. It creates a structure in which every person knows how they fit into the process and how they support those around them. It creates processes that are easy to understand and facilitates progress toward getting work done. Additionally, simple tools are developed to communicate at every level of the system, both up and down, to keep the project moving forward.

In this CQI model, looking for new opportunities to improve becomes ingrained into the day-to-day activities of the employees. It slowly morphs the organizational culture into one that is constantly looking for ways to improve.

In preparing for the semi-annual brainstorming sessions, many team members and leads begin accumulating ideas months before. This manifestation of governance and infrastructure is the cornerstone of creating a culture that sustains programs through the CQI model.

Developing an A+ governance infrastructure in an organization to implement changes is not difficult, although it does require compliance with 10 crucial steps:

1. Identifying and developing the sponsor
2. Identifying and developing the project manager (PM)
3. Creating a steering committee
4. Creating a working group
5. Creating team leads
6. Creating team members
7. Creating the project coordinator
8. Reporting functions
9. Scheduling meetings
10. Documenting meetings and sending out notes

The development of the governance infrastructure for major initiatives starts with the program sponsor. A sponsor is typically the lead executive that champions and promotes the program or project. Program sponsors are typically the recipients of the benefits or have a strong stake in the outcome. The importance of the sponsor is absolute in that barriers will invariably come up during any major initiative and senior leadership with a vested interest will be required to help move the project forward. In many organizations, this role often falls to the chief executive officer, chief operating officer, or a vice president.

Project sponsors that have control of the funds and understand the politics of the organization are great resources for leading initiatives. Unfortunately, many projects in healthcare today still operate without a project sponsor. Additionally, in many organizations, the role of the project sponsor is not well-defined, which renders it useless. Experienced PMs often think sponsors are here to shake hands at the kick-off and do the victory lap at the end. But the power of the sponsors lies in their ability to effect change and be a resource for process transformation.

It is critical that the PI leader educates sponsors on their role, expectations, and team dynamics. Sponsors often want to help but don't know how. Providing clear direction to the sponsor about what is required enhances his or her effectiveness. It is critical that sponsors have ample time to respond. There is nothing worse than asking a sponsor to help out at the last second before an impending disaster. Always provide enough lead time on issues to give the sponsor time to react. You can typically do this through steering committee updates and private conversations when issues are brewing.

Identifying and developing the right PM for any particular initiative or project is critical and is the foundation for a sustainable program. This role controls the tempo and the direction of the project. Ultimately, all responsibilities good or bad fall on the shoulders of the PM in the delivery of results. PM responsibilities include delivering every project on time, within budget and scope. PMs should have strength and understanding in business, management, budgeting, and analytics. Additionally, PMs should have the communication skills required to articulate the vision, process, status, and issues. Good PMs are skilled at getting the best out of the people and projects they oversee. They thrive when planning projects and working with project teams to achieve a purposeful outcome.

The specific responsibilities of PMs include

■ Coordinating internal resources and third parties/vendors for execution
■ Ensuring that all projects are delivered on time, within scope, and within budget
■ Developing project scopes and objectives
■ Involving all relevant stakeholders

- Ensuring the technical feasibility of the initiative
- Making sure there is resource availability and proper allocation
- Developing a robust project accountability tool to track progress
- Creating an escalation process to manage barriers
- Managing the relationship with the sponsor, steering committee, and all stakeholders

Typically, PI leaders make great PMs since they have the Performance Improvement background that is rooted in strong project management and analytics. Making sure that the PM has a good rapport with the team is critical as they all have to work together to achieve the final vision. PMs that are too abrupt or have weak communication skills will find themselves at a big disadvantage. Technical competency is no substitute in this arena as it takes the entire team to get to the finish line.

Creating the right steering committee is critical in that it is the one entity in the governance structure that has the power to effect change in the organization in multiple functions. Finding the right committee members is key to making sure that each team has a "go-to" person to help when they hit barriers.

Typically, the duties of the steering committee include ensuring that initiatives support the business goals and objectives of the organization. The steering committee is often responsible for creating working groups and choosing the right experts to complete a project. Proposed changes to a project's scope, budget, or timeline must be approved by the steering committee to ensure that the changes align with the project's aim.

The steering committee depends on tools to help them manage initiatives. This includes defining the purpose of the steering committee through a charter. The committee needs to know what their objectives and scope of powers are. Many steering committees create project charters to hold project teams accountable. Additionally, the steering committee depends on status updates through tracking systems and risk analysis tools to help them identify critical points of the projects.

The composition of steering committee membership is different for various initiatives, but generally a team of six people (give or take) is the most effective. Any more can bring decision making to a halt. Anything less and you may not have enough to make decisions. Although members can come from various levels of the organization, typically they are top-level leaders that can effect change.

One point of frustration for many PMs is sitting through monthly project update meetings only to find out that tasks have not been completed because of minor barriers that could have been resolved quickly. A new added structure called the working group is increasingly becoming the solution in many organizations to keep projects moving forward in between the formal updates. These members work alongside the team leads making sure there are no problems.

The working group is the special force of the governance infrastructure. It consists of leaders at various levels of the organization with the ability to make quick decisions and escalate issues straight to the top. The purpose of the working group is to manage the project behind the scenes and in between the meeting updates. The members remove barriers as quickly as possible, so that a process does not sit idle until the ensuing project update meetings.

The working group members partner with the team leads, who are the functional leaders that head specific areas within the initiative or project. Team leads are the owners of specific tasks and this is where the work gets done. For labor, it could be overtime or contract labor functions. For non-labor, it could be pharmacy, lab, or surgery. Identifying the right team lead is critical because at this level of the project, many of the members are working managers and need to have the motivation to do project work beyond their regular 40-hour weeks, especially if they are CQI initiatives that have no end date.

Team leads can be overwhelmed easily and may often get stuck on tasks by not understanding the request or the expectations. It is important that the PM and the working group are available to monitor and provide any required assistance. Overtime team leads may burnout, which makes it important to monitor the leads so that changes can be put in place when required. Typically, team leads are changed out annually to prevent burnout.

Team leads will typically recruit team members such as supervisors or frontline staff within their functional areas for help. This allows for the team to brainstorm ideas collectively and help divvy the tasks so that no single person is overburdened. Team members can often step in when leads are not available for meetings and also represent a pool of applicants that may show leadership qualities for future projects.

The project coordinator position is another critical part of the infrastructure for any initiative. The purpose of this position is to make sure that all the teams are compliant with the predetermined structure of the project or program and are using the proper tools. The project coordinator keeps the team leads on task and escalates issues immediately to the working group and the PM. Typical tasks include taking minutes during meetings, distributing assignments after each meeting, setting up the team meetings, attending all meetings, and reporting any issues back to the PM and the working group.

Project coordinators were originally assigned to busy vice presidents (VPs) who were managing large-scale, high-profile projects and initiatives. Senior leaders were typically very busy and were not able to manage projects on a daily basis. Thus, project coordinators became their assistants to help complete the administrative work of the project and escalate issues.

For example, a project coordinator may say to a team lead that in order to complete a task that is due by Monday of next week, they need to have two meetings set up by this Friday.

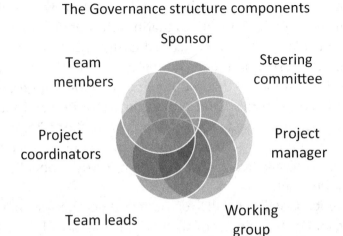

The Governance structure components

Sponsor

Team members

Steering committee

Project coordinators

Project manager

Team leads

Working group

Exhibit 5.1 The top seven components of a strong governance model.

Another example might be that the project coordinator escalates an issue to the VP prior to an upcoming steering committee meeting so that the issue can be resolved ahead of time. The project coordinators keep the project running administratively and have the pulse of the teams. They are typically the first people to know when there is team lead burnout and the root issues that may be plaguing certain teams.

By the time the full governance infrastructure is put into place, an initiative could have as many as 5–100 members, ranging from senior leaders to frontline staff. Smaller projects will consist of a PM, a working group, and a coordinator. For an example of a full-blown program structure, see Exhibit 5.1.

SETTING UP THE INFRASTRUCTURE IN 100 DAYS IN 6 KEY AREAS

II

Chapter 6

Non-Labor—The #1 Missed Opportunity in Healthcare

Opportunity is often difficult to recognize; we usually expect it to beckon us with beepers and billboards.

William Arthur Ward

To stay ahead of declining margins, US healthcare organizations have integrated several key expense reduction strategies into their routine annual Performance Improvement (PI) plans. This includes a traditionally untapped area of opportunity commonly referred to as *non-labor*. As the name implies, non-labor projects represent any aspect of expense control that take out waste unrelated to labor. Common categories of expense in non-labor include contracts, purchase services, materials management, IM, human resources, service lines, lab, pharmacy, radiology, surgery, and product utilization. Product utilization refers to the deployment of a product in a clinical setting and is considered to be the biggest untapped opportunity in healthcare today for non-labor. As most organizations are reactionary to expense control, they often lean toward labor for immediate returns, leaving non-labor overtime as one of the largest opportunities within most organizations.

Healthcare organizations have become very good at leveraging their size through consolidation and partnering with purchasing coalitions. This allows for reductions in costs through volume discounts and exclusivity contracts. Although this model has been in existence for years, organizations continue to have a significant number of contracts that are still negotiated at the facility's departmental level. Because it is very difficult to track these individual contracts, there are almost always new ways, even today, to find opportunities and negotiate with vendors. Additionally, as new products and services come online, the dynamics of vendor arrangements are kept in a constant state of flux, which presents new opportunities to negotiate contracts. We will review contract negotiation in further detail in Chapter 11.

Although negotiating new contract rates and options is always an area of opportunity, the one area that has the largest capacity to impact non-labor expense reduction is clinical utilization. This opportunity is based on evaluating the efficiency by which care is provided to the patient. Typical opportunities in utilization include provider access to best practices, workflow optimization, consolidation of protocols, standardization in supplies and vendors, and utilization management of high-cost pharmaceuticals and devices. Clinical utilization has traditionally been very difficult to break into because it involves a partnership between administrators and physicians.

We know that 80% of healthcare costs associated with treating a patient are under the control of the provider. These costs are rooted in how the provider manages various aspects of patient treatment, such as the surgery performed, devices used, length of stay, and so on. Providers are typically unaware of or uninterested in the impact of their decisions on financial costs to the patient or the organization. A recent study revealed that less than 20% of providers, including doctors and mid-level providers, actually knew what the costs associated with their decisions were. Additionally, many providers don't have benchmarks to compare their practices versus that of their peers. For example, in a recent orthopedics study, it was uncovered that the surgery time for rotator cuffs varied by more than 300% between various providers. This is just for one procedure, in one specialty. The ability for any organization to affect this variance, just by targeting the average surgery time, will have an impact that is worth millions.

Organizations can enjoy huge returns in non-labor expense reduction by following several key steps that have proven instrumental. These key features transform organizations from good to great by producing large-scale results. These include measuring correctly, developing targets, setting up the teams for sustainability, and driving accountability through leadership.

In order to begin the process of managing non-labor initiatives for expense reduction strategies, an organization has to be able to track and measure results financially and operationally. Financial measurements include Supply Cost per Case Mix Index (CMI) Adjusted Discharge and Drug Cost per CMI Adjusted Discharge. These indicators can also be measured by admissions, net operating income, or revenues. Additionally, many organizations break out implants and medical/surgical costs for more detailed accounting, opportunity identification, and results tracking.

Supply Cost per CMI Adjusted Discharge is measured by taking all supply costs and dividing it by the number of discharges for that time period (typically a month). The discharges are often adjusted for CMI in order to account for the acuity of the patients. For example, patients with a higher CMI tend to be sicker and retrospectively are more resource intensive when it comes to supplies. It is important to note that pharmacy costs are always included in total supply costs. Therefore, when breaking down total supply costs, all the parts that make up those costs, such as medical/surgical, drugs, and implants, should be listed.

Non-labor operational metrics are tightly associated with the utilization of products and services. These include average time for procedures, devices used per procedure, supplies used by provider or service line, and process efficiency indicators. Additional indicators are those associated with lab, pharmacy, and radiology, and are often tracked as a rate against discharge, patient, or admission. These indicators tend to be much more targeted at a tactical level versus general supply indicators. As the utilization of products in clinical pathways comes to the forefront of healthcare, new metrics will be developed for the measurement of efficiency and productivity.

Because non-labor can be defined broadly, there are a whole host of other metrics that can be used to measure performance. For example, if the technology department is part of the non-labor initiative, metrics such as cost per license, information technology (IT) costs per Case Mix Index (CMI) Adjusted Discharge, or net operating income can be used. The key is to use the PI function or decision support systems (DSS) to help identify measures that are relevant, available, and easy to capture. In this process, the PI function along with the team members should work together to reach a consensus on what metrics will be used and quickly lock in the baseline measures before moving forward with the initiative. In the end, if it cannot be measured, it is not worth doing.

Once the baseline metrics are locked in, the team needs to determine targets for the initiative. Targets for non-labor projects can be derived from several sources. This includes internal and external benchmarking systems and the incremental approach. There are several good external benchmarking tools being used in the industry today, including those provided by Truven Benchmarking and Premier. In this process, data is submitted, normalized, and compared against a group of peers. Internal benchmarking is predominately used by multi-hospital systems. The model is the same as external benchmarking, except that it uses internal hospitals as the compare group. The drawback of internal benchmarking is that the ability to normalize is limited and the entire system could potentially be low-performing. The incremental approach uses an arbitrary marker as a target. For example, if an organization has an average run rate of $1500 per CMI Adjusted Discharge, that could be the ceiling target. Once that target is achieved, the next average becomes the ceiling.

Once the target has been identified, a gap analysis needs to be completed so that the variance can be quantified in terms of dollars. For example, let's assume an organization with 20,000 annual discharges has a current run rate of $1500 per CMI Adjusted Discharge and their target has been set at $1300 per CMI Adjusted Discharge. The variance of $200 is multiplied by the number of annual discharges to provide the dollar opportunity. In this case, $200 × 20,000 discharges represents a $4 million opportunity in this organization.

Before a non-labor project can be kicked off in an organization, leadership has to be aligned behind it. This means getting the chief financial officer (CFO), chief operating officer (COO), and chief executive officer (CEO) to agree to mobilize the organization and hold leadership accountable to the targets. The best environment in which to push this type of initiative is one where there is a burning platform for change. Without a burning platform, motivating staff who are busy with their daily jobs will be that much more difficult. A CEO I once worked with would often say "Don't waste a good crisis." If the organization is going through financial problems, feel free to show how this initiative can help it get to its margins.

The advantage that non-labor expense reduction has over other initiatives is that it is *free*. It targets the ideas of existing staff who do the work day in and day out. As subject matter experts, these associates are the ones who can tell how to make that job more efficient. Additionally, non-labor put against revenue-generating projects has the distinct advantage in that, dollar for dollar, it has a greater impact on the bottom line. For every dollar of new revenue, only 10 cents makes it to the bottom line. Yet every $1 of cost reduction adds $1 of revenue to the bottom line. This should make non-labor not just a good project, but a great project for any organization at any point in time.

Once the CEO and CFO buy into the initiative, the PI leader or project manager (PM) must begin preparation for kick-off. The communication and kick-off for the non-labor program has two phases: executive kick-off and team kick-off. These events typically occur within 30 days of each other and require extensive amounts of preparation.

The executive kick-off should not take more than 1–2 hours based on the size of the organization. In this meeting, the CEO, CFO, and PM set the stage for the program objectives and details of the path forward. The first half of the presentation should provide the "why" behind the initiative, details of the program, and the provider-based dyad model. The second half should focus on selecting the functional categories, steering committee members, team lead names, and provider partners. During this presentation, it is important to show successes in other organizations and the expected pitfalls and opportunities.

The executive kick-off typically includes all C-Suite leaders and vice presidents. There are several critical requirements that must precipitate from the executive meeting kick-off. These include non-labor functional categories, steering committee members, team lead names, and physician leads.

Non-labor categories represent major functions within any organization that team leads would be assigned to for opportunity development including

- Ancillaries such as lab, radiology, and pharmacy
- Service lines such as orthopedics, cardiology, and oncology
- Patient services such as surgery, medical/surgical, emergency room, and intensive care units

■ System-level functions such as IT, revenue cycle, and out-patient areas

Not all facilities function the same. Therefore, it is critical that leadership identify which areas present the biggest opportunities. For example, if your IT functions are outsourced, don't put them on the team. If you have a large cardiology program, make sure to put it on the list.

Ask for about four to six steering committee members that will be comprised of senior leadership and physicians. The CNO, COO, PI, and materials manager are critical members that comprise the core group. Additionally, at least one provider should sit on the steering committee. This person could be the head of surgery or the leader of one of the product lines such as cardiology or orthopedics. The purpose of this team is to remove all barriers so that the team leads can complete their tasks. Unlike traditional steering committees, this group is much more action-oriented and will be actively engaged in helping the team leads tactically.

Team leads are critical because they are the ones doing all the work. They work with frontline staff to generate ideas, bring them to the steering committee for approval, and then begin implementing them. The expectation is that the team leads do this on top of their daily activities. Ask the leadership for strong managers or supervisors that they recommend to lead these teams. Use a tool such as flip charts to list the categories of functions that leads would be assigned to and start listing names. Additionally, it is important to find a physician lead who will partner with the team leads for each category. This process starts to get buy-in from leadership and provides the information required for the next meeting at the team kick-off.

It is important to emphasize the importance of physician involvement in rolling out a robust non-labor program. The non-labor program is at its strongest in a dyad model, which pairs administrators with providers. By forming a partnership, providers can help administrators in being physician champions for clinical projects. This is critical as the vast majority of future projects will predominately consist of utilization projects. Utilization changes consist almost exclusively of clinical processes, and without provider support, failure is imminent. This process is much simpler in organizations that have employed the doctor model versus the community-based model. In either case, physician champions have to be identified and partnered to move non-labor projects forward.

Physicians can also have a substantial impact by helping design clinical processes, providing focus for projects, and helping with accountability among peers. Most organizations do have directorships and physician champions by service line or specialty. The non-labor team needs to use these providers to help drive projects and influence other physicians. By identifying a physician champion, organizations can engage more physicians to achieve consensus. A reduction in variation reduces costs and improves quality across the enterprise.

Once the leadership understands the "why?" behind the initiative and is in support, it is time to prepare for the grand team kick-off. This kick-off is a somewhat elaborate event that can have as many as 50+ people in attendance. They include the sponsor, steering committee, working group, team leads, team members, physicians, and ancillary staff such as finance and team coordinators.

The grand kick-off is the meeting in which all members are brought together to understand the objective, structure, governance, expectations, and next steps for the non-labor initiative. It is typically a very exciting event with the CEO and physicians being in attendance. The event takes about two hours and the objective is to get everyone motivated.

In preparation for the grand kick-off, the PM should begin by identifying a project coordinator for the program. This is the person that will help with coordinating meetings, creating agendas, taking minutes, keeping teams on task, and assisting with tracking projects. The project coordinator is the one person that knows what every team is doing because they attend every meeting. This person is a great resource to provide insight about pending issues and team dynamics.

Once the project coordinator is identified, have them set up the logistics of the grand kick-off. This includes a forum that can house 50+ people, preferably off campus. Additionally, try to provide round tables so that during the brainstorming session teams can sit together. Make sure the meeting has an agenda, list of members, pads to take notes, and template to record ideas. It is always a good idea to make the meeting part of a meal, breakfast, or lunch. If you have a large number of providers in attendance, you should consider an early morning meeting. Gifts are always a nice token of appreciation for the team members at the event. Although there are lots of moving parts, the entire kick-off program should flow very naturally.

The CEO should kick off the meeting by welcoming everyone, explaining the "why," and connecting the program to the vision and mission of the organization. The PM should explain the process, structure, and governance of the program. The physician lead should motivate the providers and show collaboration with the administrative team. In the first hour, all questions about the program should be answered.

In the second half of the program, teams are divided into their groups and are encouraged to begin brainstorming non-labor ideas. Before the teams start, the PM should set the ground rules for the process. For example, ideas that are part of labor cannot be included, ideas that have been budgeted cannot be included, and ideas that cannot be quantified cannot be included. Additionally, the PM should provide each team a target dollar amount for the year. Each organization should tailor the rules to its own facility.

The steering committee members along with the PM should move around and help the teams brainstorm ideas. The PM should keep the teams on track and make sure they use the tools provided, and stay on time. Once all the ideas have been discussed and recorded in the ideas template, everyone returns to their seats. The CEO should close the meeting by thanking everyone and encouraging the teams to work together.

The team leads typically have 30–45 days to go back and refine their ideas and brainstorm further with the frontline staff. The team leads will meet weekly for the first month to generate ideas. All ideas have to be quantified and verified by the finance department. Once the deadline arrives, the team leads will present their ideas to the steering committee. Once approved, the ideas go into the tracking system and the project coordinator will begin tracking progress toward the goal. Progress is measured in two ways. The first is making sure that the project is implemented. The second is making sure the benefits are realized.

Finance has a very strong role in the non-labor team. Projects are typically given a target, which is a general number that is often based on benchmarking targets. Once the team has reviewed the opportunity and assigned actual numbers, based on actual volumes or dollars, they develop the identified opportunity. After implementation, the opportunity realized to the bottom line is recorded. All three numbers may be different. Additionally, benefits realized can be higher or lower than what was originally identified or targeted.

The entire non-labor program can be up and running within your organization in less than 100 days. Here is a detailed timeline of a typical program development.

Step 1: The preliminary work includes the development of tracking and kick-off templates, identification of baseline metrics, identification of the steering committee, and the scheduling of critical dates.

Step 2: The executive and grand kick-off. The executive kick-off is typically a 1-hour meeting to explain the program structure and objectives. In this meeting, team members are validated along with financial targets.

Additionally, this is the meeting where the CEO will set the stage for expectations and accountability from the leaders.

The grand kick-off should include the steering committee members, providers, team leads, team members, finance, project coordinator, PI, and any executives that are stakeholders. This meeting should occur within 1–2 weeks of the executive kick-off based on preliminary work and scheduling.

Step 3: This starts at the grand kick-off and continues for the next 30 days. The team should meet weekly to brainstorm and generate ideas. This step is critical and the teams require strong support from senior leadership. If the facility is part of a larger system, ideas from other facilities should be shared during this time to help team leads identify viable projects. It is important during this phase that providers are given an opportunity to interact and work team leads generate ideas.

Step 4: Once the ideas have been identified, finance should take about 2–3 weeks to validate the opportunities. In this process, opportunities have to be categorized into financial categories. These include cost avoidance versus cost reduction, fiscal year impact, and budgeted versus pick-ups.

Step 5: The report out is the final step before implementation. In this process, the team leads finalize the information and present it for final approval to the steering committee. Once this step is complete, the teams basically go into implementation mode.

This process is repeated every 6 months to keep the initiative moving forward and growing at the same time. In this model, the culture of the organization begins changing over time into one that is constantly looking to improve. See Exhibit 6.1.

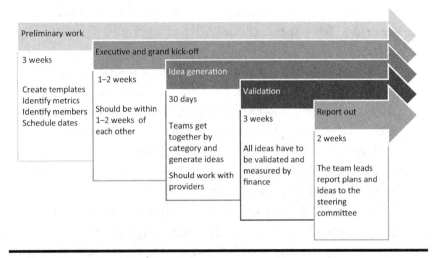

Exhibit 6.1   The non-labor 100-day roll out plan.

To encourage the teams to work hard in the brainstorming sessions, the PM will often create competition by providing dinners and gifts to teams that have the highest dollar opportunity or the highest number of opportunities identified. This process occurs semi-annually to keep the teams active and ideas flowing. After a few years, many team members quickly learn to identify opportunities throughout the year to be prepared for the semi-annual events. In this model, looking for opportunities to decrease expenses becomes part of the culture.

The tracking system for non-labor initiatives is very robust. Typically, tracking systems will include records such as

- *Task number*: This is the numbering system for quick identification of projects.
- *Project*: The projects that were approved by the committee for implementation.
- *Person accountable*: The person accountable for completing the task on time.
- *Date implemented*: The date that the project was complete.

- *Dollar target*: Initial opportunity identified without a detailed analysis.
- *Dollar identified*: Identified opportunity after detailed analysis.
- *Dollars realized*: Dollars saved during a 1-year period after implementation.
- *Fiscal year*: The year the benefits will be realized.
- *Barriers*: Issues that the project has to overcome to complete implementation.
- *Status*: Status of project against the timeline. Red/yellow/ green status report, where red represents projects that are in danger, yellow represents projects that are at risk, and green represents projects that are on target.
- *Comments*: Important comments made by the team leads for the PM.

The financial function has a very important role as it audits and verifies the savings. As the number of projects can increase dramatically in a large organization, finance often relegates to doing audits for validation. In many organizations, finance audits all initiatives that are valued at $10,000 or more as resources are limited. Finance also verifies that these ideas are real and categorized appropriately.

At the end of every fiscal year, there is always a review of the initiative. Graphs are produced that show the compilation of realized benefits against the identified opportunities. Additionally, the dollars achieved by team leads are displayed for review. Team leads showcase their accomplishments to senior executives. And with every year-end review, there is a new beginning as the brainstorming session for the new year begins.

Staff will always have reasons why they are unable to find opportunities in non-labor. These include a recent evaluation by consulting companies, being part of strong purchasing coalitions, and having recently gone through a similar initiative. No organization to date that has gone through the process just described in this chapter has ever failed to produce results. Results are tied directly to the expectations of senior leadership of their departmental leaders.

An organization in a typical facility can expect to identify a $1 million opportunity for every 150 beds. Hence, a 600-bed facility should target a $4 million opportunity from their teams. With an average number of 8 teams per facility, this represents a target of $500,000 per team. Although each team has a target, invariably some will do better than others. So long as the total dollars hits the target, the team has together achieved the goal.

Statistically, some portion of the projects will fail, so every good PM will provide a target that is slightly more aggressive. On average, about 25% of non-labor projects fail for one reason or another. By staying ahead of the target, the PM is assured of meeting any targeted expectations.

By mobilizing the organization, leadership can create a system that will begin to produce results indefinitely. Like any machine, every once in a while, work has to be done to keep the system running smoothly. This includes bringing in new team leads annually, motivating frontline staff with rewards, and keeping the meetings on task. Over time, this program can become the single most effective tool for expense reduction across the organization.

Chapter 7

Labor: Controlling Labor Permanently

> Time is the scarcest resource and unless it is managed, nothing else can be managed.
>
> **Peter Drucker**

Labor costs represent more than 50% of the annual budget in most hospitals in the US health system. This opportunity is growing based on recent increases in minimum wage and premium pay standards. Additionally, with the advent of the Affordable Care Act and Baby Boomers gearing for retirement, labor costs are expected to increase. To survive the next decade, organizations have to develop strategies that deploy the workforce in the most efficient and productive manner for long-term sustainability. Unfortunately, labor is not easy to control. There are union, city, state, and federal regulations to contend with, as well as market forces and organizational culture. Organizations that are able to navigate these barriers and design innovative labor management models will be poised for success. This chapter will provide a practical approach to managing labor in your facility.

Managing labor is a large-scale endeavor and the best approach is to employ the Performance Improvement (PI) model that breaks labor systems into technology, people, and processes. Technology represents the information management systems and tools that assist with functions such as benchmarking, staff scheduling, reporting, forecasting, budgeting, and calculating labor statistics. People represents the human factor of labor management and includes activities such as developing work standards, pay scales, benefits, licensing, and staffing to volumes. Managing labor processes refers to procedures that control the procurement and management of human resources (HR). This includes factors such as full-time equivalent (FTE) approval and outlier management processes.

Managing labor in healthcare facilities has been a very elusive task. Organizations seesaw back and forth from great to poor performance. This cycle of unsustainability has been in effect for so long that it is often referred to as the *sawtooth effect*. This phenomenon starts with limited labor control over a period of time that reaches the point of unsustainability. Then, a dramatic shift occurs that brings it back under control in a short timeframe. This shift can come in many ways, including a reduction in force. Of course, the problem is that the underlying systematic issues are not solved, and it is only a matter of time before the same positions are hired and costs rise back up and another dramatic event occurs to bring labor costs back into alignment. When tracked over time, the graph resembles a sawtooth. See Exhibit 7.1.

To manage labor, it is critical that every leader becomes familiar with the common terms that are used. Whether it is people, processes, or systems, understanding the definition and the nuances of these terms is critical. Here is a quick glossary of the terms that we will be using in this chapter.

- ■ *FTE*: This acronym stands for full-time equivalent. Numerically, it represents a full-time person at 2080 hours per year or 40 hours per week. This metric is important

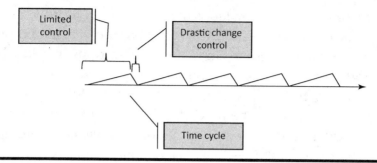

Exhibit 7.1   Graphical view of the saw tooth effect.

because a manager may use multiple part-time employees to fill various shifts. This calculation provides an equivalency of a full-time person using all the part-time employees.

■ *Overtime*: The amount of time worked that is over 40 hours per week by an employee. Typically, this is paid in time and a half, and is also referred to as premium pay. This can be paid to both hourly and exempt employees. There are several types of overtime, as follows:

  – *Scheduled overtime*: This type of overtime is typically found in organizations that are low on staff or have functions that require employees to work odd shifts, such as 24-hour flight crews.

  – *Incremental overtime*: This occurs when full-time staff punch in early or punch out late. This is an easy problem to fix with solutions such as minute-to-minute clocking.

  – *Call-back overtime*: This occurs due to staffing emergencies such as call-backs, no-shows, or terminations.

■ *Contract labor*: Labor that is contracted for a period of time. There are many companies that bring in these staff from various parts of the country. Contracted rates are typically three times the normal rate. The worst-case scenario is one where contract labor is doing overtime. The rates can quickly escalate to four or five times the normal rate.

- *Premium labor*: Any labor that is above the normal rate. Typically, overtime and contract labor are considered premium pay employees. In many organizations, weekend and holiday pay is also considered premium pay.
- *Productive time*: Also referred to as worked time, this metric represents the time the employee actually worked toward a product or service. It does not include training or bereavement, but does include daily breaks.
- *Fixed*: These are departments that do not adjust staffing during fluctuations. This is typically seen in system-level functions such as decision support, finance, or information technology (IT).
- *Variable*: These are departments that adjust based on volumes. An organization should make every effort to convert every department into a variable one.
- *Nonproductive time*: The time that an employee earns but is not used to produce a product or service. For example, the time an employee earns as paid time off or sick days.
- *Units of service*: A unit that the output of a department can be measured by. For example, a lab can use number of tests, a pharmacy can use doses filled, and nursing can use patient days. Labor statistics and ratios are not interchangeable across units of service. For example, the same departments can have completely different labor statistics when switching from patient days to discharges.
- *Worked hours per unit of service*: The productive time divided by the unit of service for a given period of time. For example, an intensive care unit can have 16 hours per patient day.
- *Paid hour per unit of service*: The total amount of dollars or hours of both productive and nonproductive time that an employee earns per a unit of service.
- *Exempt*: Employees who are salaried and whose organization is not obligated to pay overtime when they go beyond the 40 hour week.

- *Nonexempt*: Hourly positions that are eligible by law for overtime once they go over 40 hours per week. There are federal statutes that define which positions are required to be exempt.
- *Agency*: Synonymous with contract labor.
- *Foreign nurses*: Nurses that are contracted to work in the United States from countries such as India, the Philippines, and South Africa. They are typically brought in through an agency that charges a premium, although they are not as expensive as contract labor.
- *Pay period*: Typically a biweekly pay cycle.
- *Retention*: This is the opposite of staff turnover, but has the same intention. This metric measures the inefficiency associated with staff leaving an organization.
- *Per diem*: Employees that work by the day. They are typically called or scheduled as needed to supplement the existing core staff.
- *Minimum staffing*: The minimum number of employees required to keep a unit or department open. Smaller organizations with low census typically run into this issue, as they need core staffing to keep places such as the emergency room open.
- *Labor standards*: Ratios applied to determine the amount of labor to be used by a unit of service. This may be in the form of hours or dollars, and paid or worked.
- *Weekend differential*: Premium pay paid on top of the normal hourly rate to incentivize employees to pick up weekend shifts. This is typically used for nursing staff in critical-need functions.
- *Normalization*: Stripping the statistics down to eliminate noise. This process allows an apples-to-apples comparison in benchmarking.
- *Holiday pay*: Premium pay paid on top of the normal hourly rate to incentivize employees to pick up shifts on holidays. This is typically used for nursing staff in critical-need functions.

- *Part-time*: Employees who work less than 40 hours per week. The definition as set by the federal government through the Affordable Care Act defines part-time as those working less than 30 hours per week. The distinction is that part-time employees typically do not get benefits.
- *Merit increase*: This is an annual increase in pay that is typically based on performance. It is often closely tied to the inflationary rate.

When discussing labor systems, it is important to understand that they include all the various systems and tools that are used to control labor. This includes IT systems that reside in the "back office," departmental systems, and external systems such as benchmarking information. These systems, although disparate, must function in unison in order to help operators manage labor. Systems working in unison provide more than just synchronized data elements, as they also speed up information. Speed is critical in that it is required for operators to begin managing at the point of opportunity. For example, when staffing on a daily basis, knowing the volumes, discharges, and schedules of staff is critical when making decisions. When labor systems work smoothly they can deliver great reporting to help support management decision making.

Labor data consists of a combination of various metrics working together to provide a picture of how labor costs are being used and managed. This includes payroll dollars that reside in finance, hours that reside in time and attendance, and personnel data that resides in HR. Each set of data on its own does not provide a full picture. Labor systems are required to work together to provide meaningful labor statistics for operators.

Healthcare facilities have been measuring labor for decades and have developed great competency in the production of routine labor statistics. This includes metrics for premium labor, labor productivity, labor process statistics, and management accountability statistics. These metrics are measured against timelines, hours, days, weeks, and months, annually. Additionally, labor can be measured as a rate against a unit of service. This could be tests, patient days, discharges, and so on. Here are some typical routine reports for labor:

1. *Overtime by dollars and hours*: This allows an understanding of the skill mix within an area. For example, a department could use two medical assistants versus one nurse who would cost more than both. In this case, the hours may be more but the dollars would be less. For this reason, it is important to look at both hours and dollars.

2. *Contract labor*: Contract labor is the most expensive labor within the organization. These hours should be tracked closely and a separation between regular and overtime hours and dollars must be made.

3. *Labor productivity*: These are measures that show the rates at which labor is used to produce a product. These metrics are typically measured against a unit of service and have common standards that are known in the industry. These include worked hours per unit of service metrics that show the number of hours that directly impact production. An example of this metric in a lab is 1 FTE per 1000 tests. The value of this metric is that it takes away all variables, such as the Family and Medical Leave Act (FMLA) and paid time off (PTO), and looks purely at the rate of labor used. Other labor productivity statistics include paid hours per unit of service. The purpose of this metric is to look at the total dollars spent overall for the unit of output in an area. This includes PTO, FMLA, and other nonproductive hours. This metric can be looked at again by dollars and hours. This is a great metric that is typically used for fixed departments.

4. *Over-shift reports*: This report identifies opportunities that show the clocking behaviors of staff. Typically, staff tend to clock in early or clock out late for various reasons. This

metric identifies departments and people who are chronic offenders.

5. *Call-back worked*: This metric looks at the hours associated with call back. These are emergency cases where employees are called in to help. It makes great sense for critical areas, but every organization should be tracking this for possible abuse. Call-back worked should also identify which departments are providing this provision to make sure they are compliant with organizational policy.

6. *Span of control statistics*: These metrics provide information about the ratio of management to direct reports at various levels of the organization. In span of control, management refers to those that provide less than 50% of their time toward patient care. Span of control studies is reviewed every few years to look for opportunities to flatten the organization.

Management accountability labor metrics can be applied to any labor reports, although typically these are statistics that are categorized by specific leaders or functions within the organization. This could be CEOs, vice presidents (VPs), directors, managers, or departments. The purpose of these metrics is twofold: (1) to create a competitive environment between different leaders; and (2) to force each leader to account for his/her performance toward achieving the objectives of the organization. For example, this could be overtime by directors or VPs.

Once internal systems are set up to produce routine labor statistics, external benchmarks are required to identify opportunities. There are many vendors that provide benchmarking statistics such as Truven and Premier. Data is typically normalized for an apples-to-apples comparison, then compare groups are defined by facility size, acuity, and other factors, and finally all the statistics are compared against each other to identify high and low performing metrics. This can occur at a system or departmental level. Most benchmarking systems have opportunity reports that show the variances by dollars in rank order to identify the priorities. Benchmarking data is typically provided on a quarterly or annual basis.

The key to benchmarking is to make the information actionable. Benchmarking is just a report, and until it is converted into an opportunity, it remains just a report. Great managers use benchmarking to identify top performing organizations and begin the process of networking. The curiosity behind understanding how others are doing the same work better and faster is the backbone of PI in labor. The key is to change the conversation from why each department is different, to how they can change to become better. There are no two hospitals that are exactly alike, but this methodology offers a way to compare nationally and learn about best practices.

Labor systems need an information delivery system that is efficient and proactive. This includes the delivery of information in a push versus pull model. Because labor data typically resides in multiple systems with various cycles, run times, and batch processes, it is important to make the process of compilation and dissemination easy for the operators. This means compiling disparate data into a pre-selected report template with routine delivery times for operators. For example, if labor statistics are reviewed by pay period, design the finance systems to send out either the report itself or an automatic link to the report.

The "people" component of labor costs represents variables such as retention, salaries, skill mix, licensure, unions, and training. The important point to remember is that all these elements are connected. For example, retention is connected to orientation, which is connected to productivity and hours worked. Having a comprehensive understanding of these elements requires critical input from HR, finance, and operations.

Retention is one of the most important aspects of controlling labor costs. It is estimated that it costs 50% of a staff member's annual salary to recruit, hire, and train a person to fill a vacant position. Organizations with high retention rates in the twenties find themselves in an environment where in 3 years they can see more than 50% turnover in their organization. Organizations with high turnover pay a heavy price in the infrastructure required to maintain business. This includes large HR recruitment functions, training facilities, and large pools of staff to backfill these positions. Additionally, the worst part of high retention is the premium pay that is required to pay temporary staff to backfill. This includes paying overtime to existing staff, paying contractors to come in from out of town, and paying additional incentive pay to bring in staff for critical-need positions. As these costs quickly add up, organizations with bad retention quickly feel the pain of open positions.

Controlling salaries is a key part of managing labor. Keeping salaries consistent, equitable, and at market rates is critical. The HR function typically manages this aspect of labor costs, along with top management. A critical misconception is that an incremental salary increase to hire a person into a critical-need position justifies a one-time increase. Salary information always gets out; therefore, to keep consistent with staff, it is important to stay within the allowed ranges designated by HR. Other misconceptions are that those who are exempt do not get overtime. There are many positions that require overtime, even on a salary. These positions must be limited as much as possible.

Managing skill mix can provide a significant amount of reduction in labor dollars. Skill mix refers to the combination of talents required for a function or task to be completed. The application of skill mix in healthcare comes in many forms including the utilization of medical assistants versus more expensive nurses. One of the nuances of optimizing skill mix in a function is that although the worked hours may go up as you are using more people, the dollars spent actually go down. This model can artificially penalize you in less sophisticated labor management systems. Every organization should start the skill mix assessment by making sure that all staff are working at the top of their license. This means that highly compensated staff such as nurses are not doing tasks that are below their licensure. For example, a nurse at discharge should not be taking the patient to the front entry instead of the transporter.

There is a significant amount of staff movement, not just in healthcare, but within each organization. This basically means a significant amount of training and orientation hours annually in every facility. Managing orientation and training to be kept at a minimum can have a significant impact on managing labor expenses. With an average of 9 weeks of training in hospitals for clinicians, even a 2-week reduction in training can have a multimillion dollar impact annually. In recent years, many organizations have begun partnering with local education programs to start the training process before the clinician enters the organization. In this partnership, the education facility trains employees in things such as the electronic medical record system before the employee's arrival at the organization.

Another aspect of labor is the management of collective bargaining through unions. Unions are very common in healthcare facilities. This has been the case for the last 30 years as healthcare organizations experienced downsizing and financial instability. The advent of unions in healthcare has created another barrier between management and staff. Unions can provide barriers such as staffing ratios and skill mix requirements that can limit an organization's ability to manage labor. The best way to manage unions is to make sure they do not come in to your organization. Otherwise, allow the HR department to lead in this element of labor.

The key to sustainability in managing labor in healthcare is to have a set of robust processes that control and manage the flow of labor. This includes a strong governance process to manage the approval of staff for replacement or new positions, and the management of labor expense reduction strategies through a committee. Additionally, strong processes that control daily management of staffing to volumes help ingrain labor management into the culture of the organization.

Every healthcare organization needs to have a labor committee for the control and sustainability of labor management functions. The three main responsibilities associated with the labor committee are: (1) managing replacement and unbudgeted FTE requests; (2) managing new budget requests for annual budget submittal; and (3) initiating labor expense reduction strategies.

The first responsibility of the labor committee is to make sure that there are controls over replacement positions. To do this, there needs to be a tool that provides departmental labor productivity metrics, by which the committee can make decisions. Indicators that show departments operating in the red or green are perfect for assisting in the determination of whether or not to approve a position. The labor committee must track any promises made through the committee justification process. As departments justify new positions, any promises, such as a reduction in wait time for imaging services, must be recorded, tracked, and reported back to the committee in the future for compliance.

The second responsibility of the labor committee is to make sure that all FTE requests for future budgets have been fully vetted before the new fiscal year. Organizations will always experience growth in volumes or providers, so new FTEs are a matter of business. The labor committee needs to make sure that these requests have a business plan and are in sync with the rest of the organization. For example, requests for multiple quality analysts for population health and the quality department merits a review by the labor committee to possibly consolidate the position into one.

The third and most important function of the labor committee is to make sure that there are routine expense control initiatives in play through the continuous quality improvement

(CQI) governance process for sustainability. The metrics lead the discussions and set the priorities, but the culture of improvement has to be never-ending. Labor has a tendency to quickly fall back into complacency. It is the most important area that needs constant monitoring by leadership.

There are three categories of labor initiatives. Category one is the management of premium labor through the management of contract employees, overtime, differential pay, callback pay, over-shift clocking, and float pool utilization. The second category of labor projects are the bread and butter of labor management—labor productivity. Labor productivity is staffing to volumes. The third category of projects include span of control and workforce optimization. Work force optimization is the function of retooling and reassigning staff. For example, an organization may have a pool of nurses that provide education services for the rollout of an electronic medical record. Once the rollout is complete, not all those employees are required and they can be retooled for other functions such as population health.

Labor committees need to design systems that look at labor initiatives from a CQI lens. This includes implementing systems that never stop monitoring labor metrics and the dissemination of data in a transparent way. For example, using the top 10 underperforming lists in each labor metric category ensures the organization is in a constant state of improvement. Additionally, metrics by VPs and directors will always keep the leadership engaged in monitoring the metrics. Transparency in a CQI model refers to more than the dissemination of data on a routine basis to all levels of the organization. Transparency also includes providing the methodology by which the metrics were developed and targets set. Systems that take into account these variables provide great clarity and support for managers and supervisors to move the organization toward high performance.

Creating a robust governance system for labor management is the hallmark of the sustainability model. Once the technology, processes, and people components of labor are in place, a robust self-facilitating system is required to make sure that all these functions are working in unison toward a common goal. This includes hiring committees, working groups, leadership accountability, and process engineering functions. Without governance, nothing will be done and nothing will last over time. It is the lifeblood of keeping the initiative moving forward. The following is a schematic that shows the components of a strong labor management model. See Exhibit 7.2.

Leadership accountability is what drives the culture. Organizations that are not under pressure to perform at the highest levels, or have a leadership team that is accommodating to departments that are not meeting budgetary and operational targets, will never be able to adapt fast enough for the changes that are on the horizon in healthcare. Creating a culture of change and accountability is the key to making sure that organizations are nimble enough to change with their environment. Leadership accountability occurs in

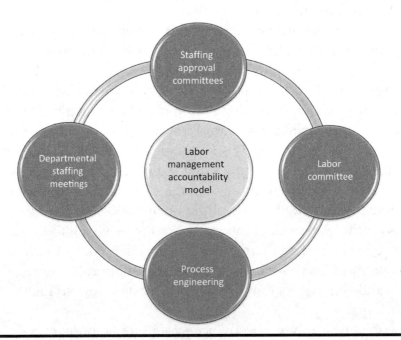

Exhibit 7.2   The labor accountability model.

both directions and is more than just beating up managers and supervisors every week over their standards and targets. Senior leaders have an obligation to provide clarity in direction, targeted operational help, and encouragement for managers and supervisors. This means helping the staff identify best practices, providing access to other leaders who have managed to find a way, and being there to monitor the environment. This support should also include PI help by assigning process engineers to help managers who are unable to find ways to improve performance. It is critical to understand that many leaders within healthcare came up the clinical ranks and are not "pretrained" managers. They may need assistance with basic management concepts such as workflow, process design, budgeting, and staffing to volumes. Leadership teams should be meeting monthly if not biweekly to review labor reports.

Departmental labor meetings should occur daily. Every variable department that is staffing to volumes should be evaluating their schedule both for volumes and staffing several times per day. This data has to be available daily to make sure that staff are able to make changes in real time. Departmental leaders have to be held accountable to their standards in biweekly or monthly meetings. Departments unable to make changes have to be assigned PI engineers to look for opportunities to improve performance.

Your organization can implement a robust labor program within 100 days. The following timeline provides a suggested implementation plan that can get the facility ramped up with all its components. See Exhibit 7.3.

Preliminary assessment of existing systems and tools: Once the strategic decision has been made to revamp the labor management process, a working group has to be created to kick-start the initiative. This group typically consists of members from PI, finance, HR, and nursing. Task one is to create a charter for the initiatives. The next step is to begin gathering information about existing committees,

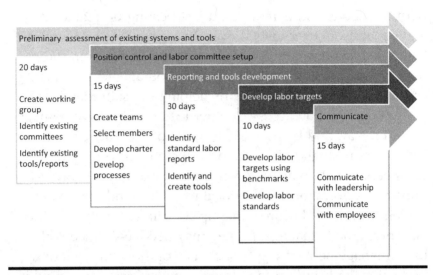

Exhibit 7.3   The labor program 100-day roll out plan.

processes, tools, and reports. In this process, a SWOT
analysis is required to identify the strengths and weaknesses of the existing systems to help guide changes.

Position control and labor committee setup: Once existing
systems have been reviewed for opportunities, the working group should begin putting together the labor control and the labor management committee. These teams
should be multidisciplinary and should be limited in size.
Often the people on the working group transition into
new roles. Other members from operational areas are
generally invited to sit on the labor control committee to
provide a forum for routine requests that come through
for approval. The labor management committee should
be the leadership team that will be reviewing reports
and holding operators accountable to their standards and
targets. The team should be composed of those who have
the authority to call in directors and even other VPs to
account for meeting targets.

Reporting and tools development: The two committees
should start by evaluating the existing processes, tools,
and reports that are in place for any required changes.

This includes changes to existing reports, the creation of new reports, and critical labor processes. Additionally, tools and reports that provide no value should be discarded. It is important to always keep in mind across both committees that the standardization of reports and tools is key.

Development of labor targets: Labor targets refer to both financial and operational targets that the organization would like to realize and the standards that will be used for volume-driven departments. Labor targets can be based on benchmarks or management observations based on existing reports. Labor standards can also be based on both, although most organizations use external benchmarking to determine labor per unit of service in order not to penalize departments that are already operating at the highest standards.

Communication: Once the committees have been assembled, and the tools developed, the organization is ready to communicate. The communication needs to occur at every level of the organization. Tools and processes have to be provided and explained to the users. Leadership has to be trained so that they can answer any questions that might come up from any associates.

Advanced organizations have departmental leaders that are very familiar with their staffing ratios and know every point when they have to add one additional person to accommodate new volumes. Often referred to as their "good and bad numbers," the staffing ratio is a reference to the point where one new additional nurse is required incrementally to take care of the next patient. As the next nurse can take care of multiple patients, department directors and managers resist until they have an ample supply of patients before they bring in the next nurse. Additionally, many organizations have developed sophisticated patient transfer systems that keep each department at their optimal numbers.

As 50% of the costs in healthcare are staff-related, managing labor is a key component of expense reduction. Creating systems that maximize the utilization of technology, people, and processes through robust governance assures the sustainability of labor controls. Providing clarity of direction, transparency of information, and support for departmental leaders to transform is the recipe for high performance.

Chapter 8

Length of Stay: Curing the Expense Disease

Why only treat the symptoms of an illness rather than cure the underlying disease?

Michael T. Rowan

Length of stay (LOS) is the single most important factor in controlling expenses across all categories in healthcare. For decades, healthcare administrators have approached expense reduction strategies from a traditional business management model. This includes the strong management of resources such as labor, non-labor, portfolio review, contracts, and supply chain. Unfortunately, this has left 80% of current healthcare expenditures untouched as the utilization of care is under the control of the providers. Because of misaligned incentives between physicians and hospitals, it has been common knowledge for years that approximately 30% of services in acute care facilities are medically unnecessary. The ability to control the medical management of patients is the newest frontier in expense reduction in healthcare and holds significant promise in reducing the cost of treating patients while increasing quality and service.

Although the medical management of patients can come in many forms, the three main areas that hold the most opportunity are order set utilization, clinical pathways, and LOS management. In the provider utilization model, a simple change in the patient treatment pattern can impact all expense categories. For example, with LOS, if a patient is discharged after 5 days instead of 7, the need for services across the organization, including labor, testing, imaging, drugs, and therapies, is dramatically reduced. Additionally, organizations struggling with capacity issues can use this model to create artificial capacity. LOS ultimately impacts every category of operations and expenses; hence, many administrators firmly believe that the biggest opportunity in the coming decade for operational optimization and expense reduction is in medical management.

The management of clinical utilization is ripe with opportunity, and requires significant provider involvement. As only physicians can write orders for admission, treatment, and discharge, they have significant control over the treatment options for a patient. Partnering with providers to identify best practices for clinical pathways or LOS is not just a good thing, it's a requirement. And providers have been, for the most part, open to working with administrators to develop mutual solutions. As an increasing number of providers turn to the employment model, the ability to reduce variation increases and the opportunity for efficiency increases significantly. Physician-owned models typically have the highest quality, service, and efficiency outcomes and are in the best position to manage clinical utilization.

Although all aspects of medical management have been under review in recent decades, patient LOS is the single largest component in the consumption of hospital resources. LOS represents the length of time a patient spends in the acute care setting during a clinical event. Typically, LOS is calculated by day using the midnight census. Patients who are admitted and discharged the same day have an LOS of zero as they never stayed past midnight. The LOS is typically compared against a benchmark target to reduce variation.

The premise behind the LOS opportunity is threefold: it increases the quality of care as the hospital can be a dangerous place for patients with falls and infections; it can improve service as patients have a tendency to feel better in their homes as opposed to hospitals that are not as comfortable; and finally it lowers expenses based on a lower utilization of services. As most hospital rates are paid based on a set Diagnostic Related Groups (DRG) rate, any costs that are avoided add to the margin for that case. Patients that stay longer than expected based on complications or other factors can cause hospitals to lose money. With an average cost of $500 per day for labor alone, hospitals stand to make tremendous profits by controlling LOS.

There are several methods of measuring LOS in an organization. LOS is typically measured as an average by taking all inpatient days and dividing the total by the number of discharges or admissions. In most cases, DRGs such as newborns are taken out. A less common method is by taking the actual time that the patient is admitted and subtracting it from the time that the patient is discharged. This number is often measured against the average CMS LOS by DRG. CMS calculates this number for all their DRGs as a geometric mean length of stay (GMLOS) to reduce the amount of variability.

Once a methodology has been derived to calculate the average length of stay (ALOS), organizations use one of two methods to track LOS performance on dashboards. The first method provides a ratio by taking the ALOS and dividing it by the GMLOS. This typically provides a number that starts with a base 1 and adjusts up and down based on the variance between the ALOS and GMLOS. The second method is where the ALOS is subtracted from the GMLOS and the variance is tracked. The variance methodology is the most accurate as it takes into account how the GMLOS is adjusting over any given time. For example, if coding is an issue, the GMLOS can increase over time. Additionally, as a ratio, it is easier to understand being a half day or quarter day above GMLOS versus having an ALOS that is a multiple of some number. Here is an example of calculations for LOS.

Organization X:

- 10,000 inpatient days during July
- 2,000 discharges during July
- ALOS equals 10,000/2,000 = 5 days for the month of July
- Assume GMLOS of those DRGs = 4.5 days
- LOS method 1 is calculated by dividing: 5/4.5 = 1.12 (ratio)
- LOS method 2 is calculated by subtracting:
  5 − 4.5 = 0.5 day opportunity

LOS is impacted by many factors during the hospital acute care episode. This includes the physiological condition of the patient, physical recovery time, and administrative and logistical functions. For the purposes of this book, it is assumed that the quality of clinical care meets all national standards of performance. Organizations with an LOS opportunity must remove every barrier that prevents the patient from leaving the acute care setting to a more appropriate level of care. Barriers can exist at any level within any function based on the variables that impact LOS. These include attending and primary care providers, hospitalists, care managers, social workers, post-acute care services, imaging, lab, pharmacy, insurers, coding, and so on.

Step one in creating a robust program to reduce LOS within any organization is to measure and assess operational performance. The simplest measure to start with is the LOS variance that was described in detail earlier. Other important measures include:

- *Discharge heat reports*: This report provides trended discharge utilization reports during any given period of time, in most cases, a 24-hour period. This is a critical report because it provides insight into the daily or weekly provider discharge patterns.

■ *Discharge by day of the week*: This report provides a count of discharges by each day of the week. The importance of this report is to provide insight into discharge patterns during the week and over the weekend. Organizations that operate 7 days per week versus 5 days per week in managing patients tend to have less peaks and valleys during the week.

■ *Discharges before 12 p.m., 10 a.m., or 8 a.m.*: This is a targeted report that strives to encourage providers and staff to push for an early morning discharge so that beds can open up as patients begin arriving from the emergency department (ED) and the elective cases in the operating room.

■ *Discharge order to actual discharge*: Many organizations have problems discharging patients after the providers have written the discharge note. This report allows management to monitor and identify opportunities where patients have not left after the discharge order has been written. This is an important indicator as nursing units often have a tendency to keep patients in beds even after the order has been written in order to catch up on work.

■ *Outlier management (outliers beyond 7, 9, 15, and 50 days)*: These reports are critical in monitoring and exploring the reasons why some chronic patients stay significantly above their normal ALOS. Patients that don't leave the acute care setting because they are homeless or require homecare are perfect examples of opportunities with outlier patients.

■ *Ancillary turnaround times (TAT) reports*: These are critical logistical reports that provide insight into internal hospital operations. TAT reports are typically provided for ancillary functions such as lab, imaging, therapies, and pharmacy. Provider consults can also be reviewed for TAT as many specialists only discharge patients by the organ in their specialty. Service level agreements are the key in managing internal ancillary service TAT.

■ *Avoidable days report*: This calculation is based on the number of days that patients stay in the acute care setting above the GMLOS for any given time period. These "opportunity days" should be categorized into buckets that represent the reasons why the organization missed those opportunities. This report is often presented in the form of a pie graph showing where the biggest opportunity is in reducing LOS.

■ *Coding response rate*: This is a key report that many organizations often skip because they forget that the variance in LOS is the problem, not just the ALOS. This metric measures the response rate of providers to coding advice for improving documentation. In this model, if the organization is able to bring the coding to the appropriate levels, the gap between the ALOS and the GMLOS would lessen.

■ *Case management patient review report*: There are many case management models in the industry today, but all of them require one key attribute. *Every patient must be seen every day.* Patient conditions change, providers change, and diagnoses change. Case managers have to be with every patient every day in order to make sure they are being managed appropriately.

■ *Provider utilization metrics*: This report tracks the utilization of services by the provider for ancillary services and the ALOS. Utilization includes therapies, consults, images, and labs. This report is predominately used to manage hospitalists within the organization.

■ *Payor response rate*: This report tracks and identifies opportunities to improve communication with insurers. Often insurance companies delay approvals for rehab, homecare, and so on. A 72-hour delay can represent a

$2000+ increase in the cost of the patient stay. This report can also be used to negotiate with insurers when renegotiating contracts.

∎ *Post-acute care response rate*: This report tracks and identifies opportunities to transfer patients to a lower level of care that is less costly. Often post-acute services such as rehab, homecare, or hospice are not very responsive to transporting patients from acute care settings, especially when they are self-pay.

∎ *Observation status rates*: Many organizations tend to enjoy high volume observation status patients because they help bring down the ALOS calculation. Unfortunately, this is a common mistake by organizations that are confused about the fact that observation patients cannot be included in the LOS calculation. Often when observation status patients are being managed appropriately, LOS has a tendency to go up as patients that used to start their stay in observation initially, now begin day one in acute care.

∎ *Departmental LOS statistics*: Every department needs to be aware of its LOS measure and its targets. Although the general ALOS is a great metric to use across the organization, departmental ALOS is critical as changes can occur incrementally at the department level. For example, orthopedics has made great strides in changing the ALOS for knees and ankles by coordinating with the providers and case management in the last decade.

These metrics should be generated routinely and disseminated automatically in a transparent manner. The time intervals for the production of these reports should be determined by the LOS steering committee. The governance teams will dictate how these reports are calculated, produced, analyzed, and converted into action items. Additionally, the LOS governance model will dictate how leadership will be held accountable to targets.

To drive LOS down, senior leadership needs to set the objectives and the direction of the organization by communicating the opportunity and the vision with clarity. Based on this vision, a mandate has to be provided to the sponsor and the project manager (PM) to mobilize the organization. Typically, the initiative sponsor begins by hiring a strong PM to begin designing the project plan and developing the governance structure. This structure is the basis for sustainability and keeping LOS low. It is inevitable that LOS will increase if not monitored and managed.

The governance structure for the LOS team requires three levels. Level one is the steering committee, which consists of—four to six members, with the initiative sponsor as the chair. Members must include the chief operating officer, chief financial officer, chief medical officer, chief nursing officer, Performance Improvement (PI) leader, and vice president of the revenue cycle. They should meet monthly to review progress and provide any general guidance for the teams. The steering committee typically focuses on large-scale changes that impact the providers, require capital investments, and are political in nature.

Level two is the working team. This is the team that gets the job done by removing barriers and making changes in real time. It consists of some steering committee members, hospitalists, analysts, and the PI leader. This is the team that reviews the data weekly, identifies opportunities, and goes after them that week. The working group is made up of leaders that have both the authority to make change and a stake in the project that will motivate them to produce results. The key facilitator in the working group is the PI leader who provides actionable data for the teams to react upon. Additionally, the PI leader keeps the teams on track according to the project plan.

Level three is made up of the functional teams that put in the day-to-day grind, including case managers, social workers, nurses, hospitalists, and technologists. As new processes and protocols are developed, these are the teams that will implement those changes at the unit level. Without these team members, nothing would get done. Team members often provide critical feedback that is important for the working group to know in implementing change. The relationship between all three levels has to be strong.

Once the governance has been developed and the membership selected and aligned with the objectives, it is time to analyze the data and develop the project plan. Typically, the PM and the working group develop the plan and present it to the steering committee for final approval. The plan should include all the tasks, expectations, and timelines, and any capital requirements needed to meet the objectives. Once the project plan has been approved, the teams are assembled for kick-off.

The kick-off for the team is meant to bring everyone together to show unity in the mission. This includes the steering committee, working group, and functional team members. All members observe what their counterparts are doing and how their work will impact the rest of the team. Data is shared in this meeting and feedback is requested about the project plan to make any final adjustments before implementation.

LOS reduction always starts by analyzing the metrics. Begin by looking at the ALOS versus the GMLOS. How far above norms is the organization? Break down the variance. What are the reasons behind this variance? Identifying a PM who has significant experience in this arena will help the organization focus in on the area of largest opportunity. As LOS is an extensive term describing many functions and processes, knowing how to prioritize will save the organization time and money.

Every organization is different and so is its performance with managing LOS. With that said, every good LOS initiative should have the following teams:

1. *Case management team*: Strong case management personnel are easy to identify. They know their provider patterns, understand patients and their families, and are

always several steps ahead of the process. They are typically more experienced nurses and can anticipate the elements that will facilitate a shorter LOS. An organization without a strong case management function is doomed.

2. *Coding team*: Not many organizations have coding leaders in their LOS teams. It is absolutely critical to have a very robust group of experienced coding nurses that review charts and make recommendations to providers. Any changes in coding can potentially increase the CMI and in turn increase the GMLOS and reduce the variance between the ALOS and GMLOS. This team constantly needs intervention as response rates from providers are surprisingly poor.

3. *Care transitions team*: This is the team that looks at transitioning from acute to post-acute care. This includes home health, rehabilitative services, and skilled nursing facilities. The ability to move patients to a less expensive level of care is critical in lowering the LOS. These teams need to monitor vendors for quality, service, and cooperation with the acute care facility.

4. *Interdisciplinary rounds team*: Typically considered the most important aspect of LOS management, interdisciplinary rounds are the key to collaboration and developing consensus in the treatment of the patient. These are daily meetings that manage the patients with all the professionals present, including the physicians. These meetings are critical and have to be attended daily.

5. *Hospitalist team*: As it is increasingly becoming the most significant aspect of LOS, many organizations are beginning to adopt an outsourced hospitalist model. This can not only help improve LOS, but also quality of care and service among patients. The secret to a great hospitalist program, whether outsourced or insourced, is to make sure that it is incentivized to help the organization meet its targets. With outsourced agencies, it is important to make sure that before any provider begins, they are given

new leader orientation that conveys with clarity what the mission and objectives of the organization are.

6. *ED team*: Every good discharge starts before the patient is admitted. More than 50% of inpatients are admitted through the ED. The ability to anticipate, place, code, and manage these patients through the healthcare process is critical. Managing patients at this point through observation, admission, and so on, can set the stage for the rest of the stay.

7. *Insurance team*: Payors are notorious for not providing feedback or approvals for patient transitions in a timely manner. Often payors have up to 72 hours to respond, which means that case managers have to start the discharge process when the patient is admitted. Having a great relationship with the payors and making sure that the contracts are not misaligned with the organizational objectives is critical.

8. *Outlier team*: When outlier patients are broken down into categories, there are always interesting opportunities and patterns. Teams have to be developed that take each category and drill down to find out root causes. In almost every scenario, the outlier teams will find that patient cases that are between 7 and 9 days typically have the biggest impact on LOS. This is the opposite of most cases where teams immediately target the highest LOS patients.

9. *Provider teams*: Changing practice patterns is never an easy adjustment for providers. These teams typically manage the difficult task of eliminating variation in the utilization of provider patterns. Physician-to-physician conversations about practice patterns are a critical part of what these teams do.

Any organization can put a robust LOS program together within 100 days. The following is a possible timeline of how a program can be set up in your facility. See Exhibit 8.1.

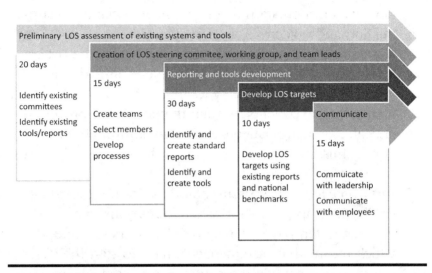

Exhibit 8.1   The LOS program 100-day roll out plan.

Preliminary assessment of existing systems and tools: In this step, the PM/PI leader must capture information about existing processes, teams, and tools that are in place so as to not duplicate efforts and eliminate efforts that are not adding value. This information has to be prepared for evaluation by the steering committee and the working group.

Creation of the LOS steering committee, working group, and team leads: In this step, the top leadership must begin the process of selecting the membership for the steering committee and working group. The working group will determine the composition of the team leads as they are operationally closer to the frontlines. The steering committee must develop the team's charter and set the expectations for the working group. The working group must in turn do the same for their team leads.

Reporting and tools development: Each governance level must review and identify opportunities to improve existing processes, reports, and tools. For example, duplicate teams must be eliminated, teams with the wrong membership must be enhanced, and tools that are not being used must be discarded or if deemed beneficial put into use. The working group will predominately lead this process.

Develop LOS targets: Once critical metrics and reports have been identified to measure key performance indicators, targets must be achieved for each team. The target starts with the most important metric, which is the variance between the GMLOS and the ALOS. Each team lead will have to develop the metrics that will contribute toward the overall LOS metric. For example, orthopedics might develop a clinical pathway to reduce its LOS from 4 days to 2.5 for hips and knees.

Communicate: To mobilize the initiative, it is critical that it is communicated to the entire organization. This process starts with the CEO providing the relationship between the mission of the organization and the mission of the initiative. Working group members must show mid-level leaders and frontline staff how their new performance targets will help drive the organization toward its goal.

Managing LOS appropriately can have a significant impact on labor and supply costs. A reduction of 1 day from ALOS at $500 per day can result in millions of dollars in opportunity. Additionally, it can enhance service and quality by putting the patients in the appropriate care setting. Taking the patient out of the acute care facility can reduce the opportunity for infections and medication errors. These benefits can be realized by your organization in less than 100 days with the proper implementation techniques.

Chapter 9

Access: Step One in Managing Service and Growth

Pioneering spirit should continue, not to conquer the planet or space ... but rather to improve the quality of life.

Bertrand Piccard

Access to healthcare is one of the most fundamental aspects of keeping a community healthy and maximizing the utilization of organizational assets. In many organizations, there are artificial barriers at every point of entry into the system that prevent patients from getting basic care such as primary, specialty, ancillary, emergency, and surgical services. This inability to get patients into the system has adverse effects on both the community and profit margins. Identifying and implementing strategies that improve access to care will enhance the health and well-being of the communities and the organizations' margins. As there are many variables that impact access, the focus of this chapter is on logistical processes such as scheduling, precertification, and physician access.

To improve access, leadership needs to remove every barrier between the patients and the services being provided by the system. To identify and understand the opportunities for improvement, organizations have to employee Performance Improvement (PI) services to map critical processes such as scheduling, precertification, and emergency room services. Additionally, key metrics have to be gathered for functions such as patient placement, transfers, days out to service, and registration for analysis and evaluation. This information combined can begin painting a picture of the opportunities that can facilitate access to healthcare.

Although access comprises many factors such as insurance, money, location, and information, the four chief areas of opportunity in access for healthcare organizations include provider appointment, emergency, post-acute, and surgical access. These four services together represent 90% of the patient experience in the acute care setting. Managing access to these services can have the largest impact that can be measured in the millions.

Primary and specialty care provider access is step one in creating access to care. If patients don't have access to basic primary care, the entire process is at risk. Primary care providers are the gatekeepers that monitor and control access to healthcare services. To make sure there is adequate access to primary care, studies have to be done to make sure the ratio of patients to providers is balanced. The typical primary care provider can have a panel of about 2500 patients. Using basic math, one can easily calculate the number of providers required to service a particular community based on its population size.

Primary care providers are increasingly being supported by mid-level providers such as physician assistants and advanced practice providers. The growth in mid-level providers has created increased capacity for routine, less complicated cases. In many states, there are rules about the number of physician assistants that can provide support for each medical doctor, but the impact has been tremendous. One advanced practice provider can add an additional 50% capacity to the existing volumes of a clinic.

Mid-level providers have also had a tremendous impact in the specialty clinics. Specialty providers in most communities have new patient appointments that are 60–90 days out in cases such as orthopedics and cardiology. Mid-levels can decrease the wait times by as much as 30%. It's important to distinguish here that for specialties, the vast majority of mid-levels treat existing patients for routine follow-up visits, creating capacity for specialists to see new patients. The specialist in turn spends most of his or her time in the most profitable sectors of the business, including the operating room, and with new patient visits.

Predictive analytics for clinic access is a new area of opportunity that provides metrics which show the impact of mid-levels on primary and specialty care provider practices. By taking the length of existing appointments for new and existing appointments, and the volumes that the providers can carry, models can be created in basic tools such as Excel to show the impact of new mid-levels. These models can be adjusted to show the ability to reduce wait times for appointments by adding an incremental number of nurses, mid-levels, or even additional providers to the practice.

Managing the physician's appointment calendar is a key component of removing artificial barriers to drive access for patients. This includes making sure that all appointments are established correctly and consistently, eliminating blocked times, and managing no-shows and cancellations appropriately. Most providers do not want to give up control of the appointment calendar and generally resist giving up blocked times, but this is step one in optimizing the schedule. Additionally, controlling no show rates by sending out patient reminder calls, and making sure that chronic offenders are incentivized not to break appointments, can increase capacity and drive access. Metrics such as appointment utilization that show the difference between appointment capacity and completed appointments quickly show wastage in existing calendar-management processes.

Call centers are increasingly becoming the more popular solution in creating an efficient access point for patients. Most hospitals have scheduling and registration functions that reside in various departments throughout the system, each with its own processes, rules, and priorities. Although the patient sees these functions as one single continuum in the course of gaining access, they are typically uncoordinated responsibilities in most hospitals. Call centers have been the solution to cut through traditional barriers and provide a single point of entrance into the system. High-functioning call centers today use robust technology with standardized processes to service all the requirements of the patient 24 hours a day, 7 days a week. Call centers can perform everything from basic scheduling to appointment reminder calls, registration, and insurance calls. Many call centers today also provide ancillary functions such as follow-up and nursing triage.

A key component of designing an access center is the technology and the staffing behind it. The technology has to bring computer systems in line with telephony. VOIP is one solution that can get your call center up and running with just internet access and a headset. The lack of a seamless process can result in operators being required to use multiple systems and analysts trying to marry up datasets for reporting. Call centers require a significant number of people to work the phones. The average hospital may have as many as 50 schedulers spread throughout the system. The only way to create a call center without breaking the bank is to identify the staff currently doing the work and reassigning them to the call center.

There are many ways to measure call center performance for access. Metrics such as speed to answer, average wait times, and appointment completion rates are typical key performance indicators that are used in call centers. Peak call times have to be monitored and staffed accordingly for optimal performance. Additionally, monitors have to be present in all areas to show wait times so that staff can log in during a rush. By keeping the call center operations optimal, healthcare organizations can be assured of improved patient access and higher patient satisfaction scores.

With new tech-savvy generations on the rise, more technology tools are being developed to provide access in nontraditional ways to healthcare. With a steady increase in video visits and telehealth every year, the new generation of patients are increasingly looking for ways to leverage technology to access care. Tools such as the EPIC MyChart application are great examples of how patients can get a direct link to their clinical information or access to their providers over the internet through the touch of a button on their phone. This technology saves patients and organizations money, and improves satisfaction all around. These systems are typically linked right into the electronic medical record.

To leverage existing technology such as the EPIC MyChart system, organizations have to show the value of these systems to the patients and to the employees. For example, if registration staff see that patients can preregister themselves and pay bills online, which will in turn reduce their workload, they would be much more apt to inform the patient of this free tool. Patients seeing the convenience of direct 24-hour access to their clinical records and providers would not hesitate to use this technology. It is suggested that at least 50% of all patients that enter the organization would use this technology if it was offered. This technology is typically promoted heavily in provider offices, although hospitals are increasingly using this technology in the inpatient setting.

Monitoring and managing outgoing provider referrals is a critical component of ensuring that all patients have adequate access within your system. Many organizations today have hospital-owned primary and specialty care providers. Monitoring the outgoing referral rates is a critical component of keeping patients within the organization. Outgoing referrals have to be routinely monitored to understand the reasons why they are being sent out. Reasons based on process and communication issues have to be systematically resolved. In cases where the patient is required to go outside of the system because of insurance, continuum of care, or specialty needs, they must be respected and possibly put on the long-term strategy list.

Patient convenience is a significant factor in providing patient access in healthcare. Increasingly, there is a great shift in the utilization of clinical services from large acute care facilities to local outpatient's clinics for routine outpatient procedures and urgent care needs. This trend has been in play for the last decade and is picking up steam with the recent explosive growth in local free-standing emergency departments across the country. The convenience of pulling into the parking lot and being within 50 steps of all your medical services is quite enticing. Providing facilities strategically around the community as access points and possible feeder systems for a higher level of care into acute care facilities should be an important part of any organization's strategy and capital investments.

Healthcare organizations are constantly changing staff, departments, processes, and providers. These changes put patient access to services at constant risk. Developing a strong governance structure to improve access is critical for sustainability and continuous quality improvement. Because of the nature of the problem, the governance structure for access does not have to be as comprehensive as other initiatives. Key components of the access governance structure include the sponsor, the working group, and team leads.

The sponsor has to communicate the vision of a single coordinated system that provides patients access to every level of care from ambulatory to acute to post-acute seamlessly. The initiative sponsor is typically a physician leader with enough clout to mobilize other primary and specialty providers to change their operations. This includes opening up their schedules, changing their appointment types, and taking operational measurements. Additionally, the physician sponsor has to have enough clout to work through the barriers between the acute and ambulatory organizations to provide a single seamless experience for the patient. This includes seamless access to primary, specialty, acute, post-acute, and follow-up care.

The working group is predominately made up of leaders from the call center, nursing, PI, and clinic operations, as well as the hospital chief operating officer and a physician leader. This team is tasked with removing barriers and keeping the project on schedule. The working group communicates instructions to directors and monitors progress through robust leading and lagging indicators. Leading indicators are metrics that measure the success of the project itself. These include metrics such as the number of people signed up on MyChart and number of people calling about an advertisement. Lagging indicators are metrics that show the final outcome of the initiative. This includes metrics such as the number of new appointments and the number of new procedures. Ultimately, the buck stops here if there is no progress in the project.

The team leads are the staff that operationalize the best practices developed by the working group. This is where all the work gets done. They bring the departmental and clinic teams together to explain new processes, implement best practices, and train the employees in the new processes. Without this group, the working team would never have the time to implement all the changes that are required to maintain great access for patients across the enterprise. It is important to note that these teams are created for acute, post-acute, outpatient, and ambulatory services, as access cuts across all these functions.

A major point of opportunity for patients accessing healthcare are handoffs from one department to another and from one organization to another. Patients often drop out within the organizational processes, moving between all the different functions that are required during routine stops such as registration, precertification, scheduling, therapy, nursing, labs, imaging, pharmacy, and so on. Typically, there are minimal processes in place that coordinate between these disparate departments. Additionally, there are a significant number of patients that drop out of the process when leaving one organization and accessing another, such as going from acute to post-acute or ambulatory care. Healthcare has attempted to put people, processes, and technology in place to keep the system moving in unison, but a good patient transition is still the exception.

Patient navigators, social workers, population health nurses, and case managers are a few examples of staff hired in both acute and ambulatory organizations to maintain the patients' access to care during transition. Patient navigators and case managers are typically those that help the process within the acute care organization. They manage the patient through both administrative and clinical functions from the time they enter the door to the time they leave. Social workers and population health nurses typically help patients navigate pre- and post-acute care. They facilitate making physician follow-up appointments, post-acute care appointments, and other functions such as pharmacy, imaging, and lab follow-up appointments. Making sure that key figures are waiting at each point of handoff to facilitate the transition is a key component of keeping the patients in the system.

Managing patient throughput within an organization is another key component of providing access to patients. Some key indicators of bottlenecks within the acute care process that prevent patients from being able to enter the system are "left without being seen," "diversion hours," and "ICU holds." It does not take long to see patients leaving the system because they cannot get in. This is a great opportunity for PI functions to analyze workflow and conduct time studies to optimize the patient throughput process from the emergency room to discharge. By eliminating bottlenecks that prevent smooth patient flow, capacity is created to allow patients into the system.

Setting aggressive patient access targets should be a part of every organization's strategy. Some access metrics are tied into pay-for-performance and quality models that can literally cost an organization money for subpar performance. This includes service scores that measure time to see the provider, and clinical quality scores that measure Medicare patients being seen by primary care providers within 7 days of an acute discharge. Other metrics such as third next available appointment should be set for specialties at no more than 10 days out and primary care at no more than 5 days out for new patients. The time to answer a call in a call center should be less than five rings. Abandoned calls should be less than 2%. Preregistration should be 95%. These metrics in totality provide a clear picture of how access is working within your organization and the priorities that need to be set for high performance.

Integrated delivery systems such as ProMedica Health System are in a great position to provide optimal patient access. Often called turnkey systems, these organizations are both horizontally and vertically integrated and can provide all the services a human might require from cradle to grave. This includes everything from primary, specialty, acute, post-acute, hospice, and insurance coverage. As integrated delivery systems typically have a single technology platform, information management is optimized as everyone has access to the same record for all instances of care. Additionally, there is communication across traditional barriers so the patients are treated at the most appropriate level of care.

There are many opportunities within organizations that provide primary and specialty care services to keep patients in the system. Primary care visits should be rescheduled before the patient leaves the office at checkout. Specialty services should be scheduled or patient's information passed along to the specialist to keep the patient in the system. Patients that require imaging or lab services should take care of that within the facility prior to leaving. This provides great service to the patients by not requiring an extra visit. The facility must make every effort to remove all barriers to entry for patients into the organization.

The following is a suggested 100-day timeline to implement a robust access initiative within your organization. See Exhibit 9.1

> *Preliminary assessment of existing systems and tools for access*: Although most organizations do not tend to have initiatives centered on access, it is important to still take an inventory of existing projects and teams to make sure there is no duplication. Existing standards and processes have to be identified as the new program is being designed for implementation. Places to look are facility call centers, patient transfer centers, and scheduling departments.
>
> *Creation of access working group and team leads*: Access centers need a strong working group to implement and roll out various programs. In this step, the PI function along with the project manager should work with senior

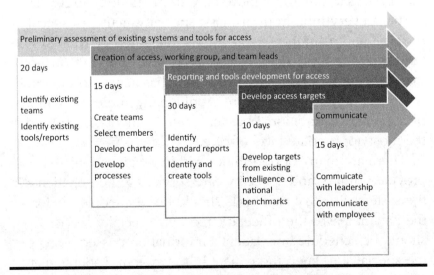

Exhibit 9.1   The access program 100-day roll out plan.

leadership to identify the best members for the working group. The working group should typically be comprised of vice presidents and directors from clinics, scheduling, patient transfer, and the operating room. The working group should in turn identify the best candidates for team leads for the expected tasks.

Reporting and tools development for access: The working group should work diligently to identify pertinent metrics that can be used to measure progress. A reliable source has to be identified that can provide these metrics on a routine and consistent basis. The team should work diligently to lock in the baseline metrics so that as process and system changes are implemented, the outcomes can be measured. For example, the existing number of transfers, patients per day by primary care, calls per day, and surgeries per day have to be measured and documented before changes are implemented.

Develop access targets: For every point of access within an organization, the working group should find an optimal target. This includes everything from provider offices to the acute care facility to call centers. For example, can new patients be seen by a provider within 5 days? Are all phone calls answered within three rings? Is the call abandonment rate below 3%? What is the average number of cases per day, or wait times for ancillaries? Once these targets have been developed, they should be put next to the baselines to identify the gaps.

Communication: To mobilize the organization toward these new access targets, the working group should put a communication plan together for every level of the organization. The CEO must connect the mission with the initiatives, the working group must connect the targets with the objectives, and the team leads must be the frontline cheer leaders who get the departments excited and engaged.

Access to healthcare is one of the most fundamental aspects of keeping a community healthy and maximizing the utilization of organizational assets. It is incumbent on every leader to remove all the barriers between patients and the care being provided within the organization. The key is to start with basic processes such as primary, specialty, ancillary, emergency, and surgical services. Over time, organizations can migrate toward more complex opportunities such as working with insurers, collaborating with government programs, and vertically integrating the system.

Identifying and implementing strategies that improve access to care will improve the health and well-being of communities and organizations' margins. By following the aforementioned implementation timeline, any organization can be on its way toward maximizing its assets and improving access to care for its communities within 100 days.

Chapter 10

Optimizing the Revenue Cycle Process

> The billing process is the first and last encounter
> patients have with a healthcare provider or hospi-
> tal. The ease and timeliness of this process has an
> incredible amount of influence on patient satisfaction.
>
> **Emad Rizk, MD**

The healthcare industry is under tremendous pressure to
improve the quality of care, while simultaneously facing
declining reimbursements and margins. In an effort to increase
revenues and improve operations, many leaders have shifted
focus to financial functions as an opportunity. It is estimated
that up to 25% of bills are rejected by CMS and more than 50%
of those are never refiled. This represents a significant loss of
revenues from improper billing. Optimizing revenue cycle efficiency and improving the areas of medical billing, coding, and
accounts receivable management are critical in staying financially viable in the next decade.

According to the Healthcare Financial Management
Association, the revenue cycle process includes all the administrative and clinical functions that contribute to the capture,
management, and collection of patient service revenue.

Based on this definition, the process begins at the point where a patient account is created and ends at the point when the balance has been satisfied.

Hospital revenue cycle systems include both clinical and administrative functions related to the generation, management, and collection of patient care revenue. In the past, these functions were often referred to as back-end functions, such as billing and collections. Today the system is focused on both the back end and the front end, including patient scheduling and registration, insurance verification, and preauthorization, as well as the core tasks of the revenue cycle including medical documentation and coding.

The growth in revenue cycle management functions precipitated from the interconnectivity of the process that links the front-end functions to the back-end functions. Any defects in the process on the front end would have a severe impact on the back end, causing rework, lost revenues, and delays. Here is a list that shows the revenue cycle process from the front-end to the back-end functions.

- *Registration*: In this process, basic information about the patient is gathered. This includes name, address, date of birth, allergies, chief complaint insurance, and any co-pays. The vast majority of the information is collected at this point. Any breakdown in the process at this point can spell disaster downstream. The vast majority of registration errors occur because the systems are not integrated or because it is simply too hard to capture all the information. This process is compounded if the patient is incapacitated. The solution is to have a process that is easy and automated.
- *Scheduling*: In this process, the patients are given an appointment time and date for services. This function is critical in that it can create serious patient bottleneck issues if done incorrectly. The scheduling function is the

tool that is used to take out the variability in wasted time for the providers and staff.

■ *Insurance verification*: In this process, the insurance information provided during registration is verified. The data captured at this point in the process is critical in that insurance companies are very detailed about when a member is covered and for what items. It is critical that the verification clerk check the information for the date of service every time.

■ *Co-pays and deductibles (up-front collections)*: These are financial obligations that are paid by the patients as a requirement of the insurance company. As more and more of the financial burden is put on the patients, it is important to collect all the cash up-front, if possible prior to the date of the service. There are two critical processes: (1) know what the patients owe; and (2) be ready to make alternative payment plans.

■ *Collections*: This is collecting the balance of the procedure from both the insurer and the patients. As claims age, the level of reimbursement is reduced, so a robust collections process can easily represent millions in savings.

■ *Documentation*: Often referred to as clinical documentation improvement (CDI), clinical documentation is defined as the creation of a digital record that details a medical treatment, clinical test, or medical trial. By documenting appropriately, a permanent record of events is created and provides the basis of the billing process. Making sure that the process is optimized and not maximized is the key. Avoiding errors in this process is critical in making sure that money is not lost.

■ *Coding*: Coders convert medical terminology into a nationally standardized format that allows the information to be transmitted between healthcare providers and insurers. Coding is a specialized function that requires knowledge of medical anatomy, patient health environments, and drugs to determine the optimal codes. The coding process recently went through a major overhaul that included a transition to ICD-10.

■ *Bill review and charge entry*: After the codes are created from the documentation, the claim is sent to medical billing for the charges to be entered. Key points to ensure include: (1) the bill is clean and has been scrubbed before it is sent out; (2) the charge master is up to date; and (3) the time from service to dropping the bill is minimal.

■ *Patient statements*: These are the typical statements that go out to the patients who must cover their portion of the responsibility. Not having a robust process can cause delays and reduced payments. Key opportunities include: (1) creating easy-to-read bills; (2) ensuring the bill goes out on time and is delivered on time; (3) providing services for patients that have questions about their bills; and (4) creating consolidated bills so that the patients are not confused.

■ *Contracting*: This includes trending and managing collections data for negotiation purposes, making sure that insurers are complaint with contract stipulations, and verifying charge data.

■ *Account receivables (AR)*: This represents the collective processes that accrue expected payments. Managing the systems, up-front collections, and denials is critical in keeping a robust AR process. This process is compounded by complexity in technology, payor contracts, and process interconnectivity.

■ *Denials management*: Denials management is a routine part of the revenue cycle process. Creating countermeasures is the key to making sure you are ahead of the insurers. This includes making sure that you have access to real-time analytics that show potential root causes and the viability of various approaches. Staff should be properly trained and motivated to aggressively go after denials.

Revenue cycle transactions can represent significant sums of money in the US healthcare system. Hundreds of millions of charges and collections may go through a facility annually. A small change in any revenue cycle process can yield significant results. For example, in a typical 500-bed facility, an organization can expect about $500 million to $1 billion in revenues to go through the system. A 1% improvement in collections can represent $5–$10 million in opportunity. The revenue cycle leader should be prepared to identify at least 10 initiatives in the revenue cycle annually to improve collections.

It is important that the revenue cycle systems be under constant scrutiny for optimization. It is important to use the word optimization as opposed to maximization when discussing revenue cycle processes because of past history with organizations up-coding to increase reimbursements artificially. In this process, the coders would chronically code higher for more reimbursement although the documentation did not warrant it. Hence, we always say that organizations deserve every dollar that they worked for, nothing more and nothing less.

Using a robust single technology platform is important in making sure that all the revenue cycle processes are fully monitored and audited for opportunity. Whatever the technology, it is important that all the activities in the process are being documented, processed, and measured on the same platform. Many organizations have disparate systems for scheduling, registration, billing, and coding. The amount of integration required to bring these silos together would be cost prohibitive. An integrated system can also enhance patient self-serve functions that allow patients to schedule appointments, complete online registration information, and even pay bills on the internet. Other advantages include assimilating core revenue cycle tasks, such as the documentation of patient care and medical coding, for appropriate billing and claims collection at the back end.

The revenue cycle teams are so specialized in their functions that projects in this area are typically led directly by the revenue cycle leader. The leader of the revenue cycle functions often brings in a Performance Improvement (PI) function or outside consultants based on the nature of the activities to identify opportunities. Either way, it is important that the revenue cycle stay under constant scrutiny for improvement.

Highly trained and motivated staff are critical in making sure that the revenue cycle process works appropriately and every effort is made to enhance revenues. This means investing so that staff are trained, equipped, and in some cases financially motivated to care about collections. Minimum wage staff in charge of millions going through their hands daily become numb to the process. Forgetting to follow up or a data entry error can cost thousands of dollars. Coders in particular have to stay trained in the latest changes and techniques.

Point-of-service collections are increasingly becoming a very important part of the revenue cycle process. As an increasing portion of the financial burden falls on the shoulders of the patient through co-pays and deductibles, being able to collect at the point of service becomes super critical. Patients may have to pay upward of $5,000, possibly even $10,000, in deductibles. This is the opportunity to collect something and look for alternative methods of payment including installments. Additionally, if beneficial, this might be an opportunity for the patient to meet with a financial counselor. It is very difficult to collect thousands on the day of surgery as a cancellation could mean wasted resources and an upset provider. Improving point-of-service collections and decreasing delays in patient billing can improve revenue cycle productivity.

CDI is an area that has significant potential. In this process, nurses familiar with coding and documentation provide input for the provider to confirm the documentation. Typically, these teams use software that allows them to access the Electronic Medical Record and then communicate with the providers about possible anomalies. The process itself has to always be under evaluation. For example, one organization realized that only 10% of the cases were being reviewed, with a 4 to 1 return. In this case, for every person brought in, there is a 400% return on that investment. In another organization, the providers were not responding to the queries of the CDI case managers. Once it was escalated to leadership, the providers started to respond to the queries. As documentation became more robust in the organization, the case mix index slowly inched higher.

Although revenue cycle projects should be handled by the functional leader, the project management office (PMO) should track and update constituents on the progress of those initiatives. Measuring revenue cycle improvement is very difficult to do. Unless the improvement is in an area that has baseline data, it is very difficult to prove that the project was responsible for any changes. Typically, most PMO functions use the budget as a benchmark to determine if the revenue cycle has improved.

The PI function can also provide support through workflow analysis and staffing opportunities for the revenue cycle teams. Additionally, the PI function can help design dashboards with key performance indicators. For the revenue cycle, these include: percent preregistered, point-of-service cash, registration error rates, charge capture, day out to code, accounts receivable (AR) over 60, 90, and 120 days, AR balance, cash days on hand, claim rejection rate, credit balance turnaround, denial overturn, and gross days receivables outstanding.

There are several major reasons for claim denials. These include patient ineligibility, incomplete patient or plan information, missing supplemental attachments, incomplete service information, duplicate claims, claims submitted to the wrong payor, and coding errors. All these mistakes can be fixed relatively easily with some oversight of claims submission. Organizations with a robust claims processing function can expect to have less than a 5% error rate in the first pass at submission.

Options to improve quality and reduce expenses in the revenue cycle process should include outsourcing the function. There are many organizations today that provide revenue cycle functions from scheduling to denials processing. These organizations have economies of scale and provide core competencies that may not exist within smaller facilities or medical practices. The staff are typically cross-trained and have significant coverage capabilities based on the size of their operations and labor force. It is no surprise that even large facilities such as Catholic Health Initiatives with over 100 hospitals outsource their billing functions to third-party vendors.

In developing the revenue cycle program, it is important that the right infrastructure and governance is put into place to maximize performance. This includes a working group that should be led by the revenue cycle vice president (VP). The working group should also include leadership from revenue cycle functions such as CDI, contracting, AR, billers, and coders. Other members that can add value to the organization include PI for project tracking and workflow management purposes. PI can also help with staffing the functions and developing dashboards for monitoring.

Functional leaders should have team leads that help bring staff together to brainstorm ideas and select projects that have the highest value. Additionally, the team lead will be tasked with implementing any changes as a result of these projects. Some projects may require an investment such as new technology or staff. The PI function should work with finance and IM to develop a pro forma to calculate the feasibility of suggestions that require investment. The working group should meet monthly and the team leads should meet every 2 weeks to review progress. Team leads need to have the express understanding that they should not wait until the monthly meetings to bring barriers to light. To enhance the communication process, a working group member has to be assigned to each team lead for problem escalation purposes.

In the absence of a PI engineer, the program must provide a program coordinator to keep the process moving. For sustainability purposes, a continuous quality improvement process will always be used to keep the program on track by making sure that problems are escalated, results are communicated, and tasks are being completed. Once the process is moving forward, a program coordinator can take over the process, which will free up the PI engineer to help with other initiatives.

A suggested timeline of events is shown in the following graph to demonstrate how quickly this process can take shape. This includes all the steps required to go from conception to implementation.

Step 1: A working group must be created and the project charter developed. This includes objectives, scope, resources, timelines, potential risks, and success metrics. Once the charter is developed, baseline metrics have to be measured and locked in as the current state. Baseline metrics must be identified and locked in before any changes are made. The step is typically completed by the PI or the project manager (PM).

Step 2: Team leads are selected and a grand kick-off is held that gets the teams excited about the initiative. Typically, the VP of the revenue cycle will lead this initiative by selecting the team leads, and getting the teams excited about the objectives. The PM/PI functions can help the revenue cycle leader track the project and provide any process evaluation tasks.

Step 3: The teams can use the next 45 days to develop ideas and solutions for identified opportunities. Additionally, this is the time when the teams can validate the targeted opportunity and verify the baselines. An important part of this step is to make sure the teams provide the "ask" for the returns they plan to provide through this initiative.

Step 4: In the final step, the PM or coordinator will set up the initial meetings and set the cadence to begin moving the process forward. See Exhibit 10.1.

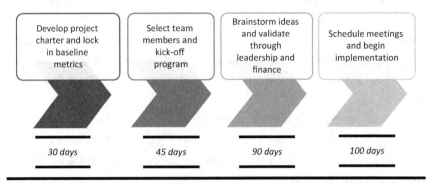

Develop project charter and lock in baseline metrics	Select team members and kick-off program	Brainstorm ideas and validate through leadership and finance	Schedule meetings and begin implementation
30 days	*45 days*	*90 days*	*100 days*

Exhibit 10.1   The revenue cycle program 100-day roll out plan.

Revenue cycle management is a high-yield frontier in improving patient satisfaction and increasing the bottom line by collecting all that the organization is owed—nothing more and nothing less. All organizations serious about expense reduction and revenue enhancement must have a high-performing revenue cycle function.

Chapter 11

Getting Comfortable with the Uncomfortable

Start out with an ideal and end up with a deal.

Karl Albrecht

Vendor contracts represent about a quarter of a typical healthcare facilities expense structure. A 500-bed hospital in the United States may have more than $100 million in contracts paid out annually. This includes supply chain, consulting services, maintenance agreements, construction, and purchase services. Many organizations target contracts as a priority for expense reduction because they are considered easier to go after in comparison to such areas as labor or clinical variation. Additionally, the impact is felt much more quickly than most other expense reduction initiatives. Any organization serious about staying ahead of the expense reduction curve should have a robust program that manages contracts through a continuous quality improvement (CQI) approach.

Third-party vendors are experts at negotiating great terms for themselves. They are flexible, creative, experienced, and have developed powerful techniques that make sure they have every advantage over you. In 2007, a study performed by

ProMedica Health System did a "year in review" of the benefits realized from a pharmaceutical drug negotiation initiative. The results were stunning in that pharmacy spend had actually increased. As the Performance Improvement (PI) team negotiated drug prices down, other prices continued to go up. This cat-and-mouse process of reducing prices in one area and raising in another was evident in a recent highly publicized case regarding Epi Pens. The price of a two-pack of Epi Pens increased by more than 500% in the last decade, rising from $100 to more than $600. Any organization that does not have a process that is perpetually negotiating and monitoring contract terms will fall behind very quickly.

Contracts in most healthcare facilities reside in multiple areas within the organization. Examples include supply chain contracts in materials management, consulting and ancillary within operational functions, and technology and construction at the system level. Most departments have developed relationships with company representatives and vendors and typically don't want to give up control over the contracts. When formulating the project working group membership, it is critical to use a multi-disciplinary approach by utilizing a combination of leaders from all these areas.

The governance and infrastructure required to renegotiate contracts should consist of a working group composed of a project sponsor, four to five negotiators, a project coordinator, and departmental subject matter experts (SMEs) as required. The project leaders will have to work closely with the materials management (MM) leader and the department leader, who have intimate knowledge of the vendor and service history. The following is a breakdown of the role of each person on the team:

- *Project sponsor*: This role is constantly in touch with working group leaders to remove barriers. Typical barriers include getting the department leaders to work with the contracts working group to get results. This person has to operate at a high enough level to exert control over departmental leaders. Additionally, the sponsor will be the final person with authority to approve or reject the terms of the contract when vendors get creative. The project sponsor should have an active role in the process and should be updated by the project manager weekly or biweekly.

■ *Working group leaders*: These leaders are handpicked by the sponsor to negotiate the contracts. This team has to be able to pick up the phone and cold call the vendors to ask for concessions without any hesitation. These negotiations could turn into uncomfortable high-pressure meetings, which requires strong character.

■ *Materials management leader*: This leader is typically the most experienced in negotiating with vendors. This person knows the tactics and generally has a standardized process to negotiate. The MM leader should be the guide for all the other team members in creating a template to use for managing negotiations. Additionally, this person would know what the constraints are associated with existing contracts and group purchasing organization (GPO) commitments.

■ *Department leaders*: These leaders are generally the owners of most contracts and considered the subject matter experts. Their role is to help facilitate the negotiation process and provide information that would be useful for the working group. Often the SMEs may want to take on the negotiation role with the vendors.

■ *Project coordinator*: The project coordinator manages all the meetings, minutes, and follow-ups, and tracks accomplishments. The coordinator keeps the process moving and quickly escalates problems identified in meetings to the leaders. Additionally, the project coordinator makes sure that new agreements are carried out.

The teams typically meet biweekly and should be negotiating at least two to three contracts per week. The project coordinator should keep minutes and distribute all the action items within 24 hours of each meeting. All barriers, next steps, and costs identified should be recorded with a report to the working group at the beginning of each meeting and monthly to the sponsor.

The first step in divvying the work among the team members should be to take inventory of all the contracts. Some organizations have a contract management system that tracks all contracts in a single system. This is typically the exception, so prepare the groundwork by identifying the location, the owner, and the dollar value of the contracts. Several methods could be used to identify contracts. Finance may track within the budgeting process, or the accounts payable team may be able to run a list of the payments made to vendors on an annual or monthly basis. Otherwise, the sponsor can always send an e-mail out to all the departments asking for a list of contracts. One way or another, an inventory of contracts must be compiled to begin the contract management expense-reduction project.

The contracts should be prioritized to maximize the highest value for the effort. For example, many organizations start by targeting all contracts that are over $1 million. This list is typically much more manageable, and only a few percent change in the terms can yield significant results. Once these contracts are complete, then the team can move to those between $500,000 and $1 million, and so on. The trick is not get overwhelmed, since organizations can have thousands of contracts. In this process, it is important to also have the ability to prioritize contracts that have upcoming due dates. This is important, as those will be the easiest to negotiate. With all contracts, not only are the renewal dates important, but so are the notification dates. This is a tactic that vendors often use to get an additional year of fees by requiring a notification period prior to the termination date.

The best results come from negotiations that team up the MM leader, the working group leader, and the departmental leader in each meeting. A typical meeting would start with the departmental leader introducing the team members and the purpose of the call, the working group leader explaining the situation and their objective, and the MM leader providing opportunities to change the terms. The coordinator should be taking notes so that the team can regroup and know the position of each side for the next meeting. When attempting to re-renegotiate terms, it is important to let the vendor know what prompted this special event. It is amazing how often vendors understand and work with their clients to reach consensus.

The working group should have a target that they are planning to achieve by renegotiating and eliminating contracts. From a PI perspective, most organizations tend to achieve a 5% opportunity based on various factors. So, if an organization has targeted $100 million of contracts, the teams should be targeting $5 million in opportunity, or 5% of each contract. At first glance, this may seem an insurmountable task, but there are many reasons why these targets are achievable. For example, contract management could also mean contract termination, which can have a significant impact on your overall spend. Even though some vendors may not negotiate, others will, and if you cancel a few contracts, the total amount goes toward your target.

To get the best deal possible, the working team has to be prepared going into negotiations. To make sure that all discussions are consistent and every opportunity for savings reviewed, it is important that the team develop a working template. This template is a script for knowing what things to ask about and to bring up during negotiations. The following is a list of negotiating tactics that you should include in your template:

- Break the contract down into its components.
- Identify unmet service level agreements.
- Ask about discounts for paying in advance.
- Inquire about discounts for extending the contract dates.

- Ask about concession to make payment by credit card that pays back.
- See if there are opportunities combining contracts for more concessions.
- Ask about volumes discounts to expanding contract into more facilities.
- See if the vendor would consider not raising charges at the normal rate.
- Ultimately just let the vendor know the situation the organization is in and why you need a discount.

Exhibit 11.1 is an example of a working template that should be used by the team to track vendor negotiations and financial outcomes.

Negotiators must change their mind-set to think about the value of the services or product versus its price. This change in philosophy looks at every opportunity for improvement and seeks every advantage for the organization. For example, an organization may be able to get better service level agreements, more licenses, or a shorter contract duration for the same price. These are all contract terms that provide value

Contract template:

Demographics				Negotiation points?		
1	Vendor name:			1	Contract Price	
2	Vendor representative:			2	Licensing terms	
3	Vendor contact information:			3	Net 30 payment	
4	Facility contract owner:			4	Payment by credit card	
5	Facility contact information:			5	Should this contract exist?	
				6	Contract extension	
Contract information				7	Contract expansion	
1	Contract duration:					
2	Contract notification time:			**Financial impact**		
3	Contract start date:			1	Target opportunity	
4	Contract amount:			2	Negotiated opportunity	
5	Scope of contract:			3	Realized opportunity	
6	Multi-year contract:					
				Status		
Leverage points				1		
1	Contract parts			2		
2	Issues with the existing contract?			3		
3	Timing			4		

Exhibit 11.1   Contract negotiations tracking template.

for the organization. Although price is the most sought after, terms can be just as good.

Cost avoidance is another opportunity for most organizations in renegotiation contracts. This opportunity can precipitate in many forms, although the basis of it is to avoid pending increases in the terms of the contract. For example, technology contracts often have a time period over which increases in transactions are measured to change the fee rates. By extending that time period over which the transactions are measured, they delay the time that additional payment may have to be paid.

Always try and leave the negotiations on a positive note. At the end, your organizations needs the services from the vendors, and each vendor has a right to make a profit to stay alive. Negotiations should be treated as a win–win and not a win–lose process. It's important to keep the drama out of the process and discuss the facts and what is practical. Negotiations typically progress much better when each party feels good about the deal and wants to make it work.

Larger healthcare organizations with corporate offices may want control over the contract negotiation process. Organizations consolidate to gain economies of scale; therefore, it is completely appropriate to yield to larger opportunities at the corporate level. Although they should be involved in many cases, there is a multitude of contracts that are negotiated and managed at the facility level that should be included in the initiative and managed appropriately. Facilities should not be surprised if their costs go up after corporate negotiates with vendors, as they are looking at the overall picture of the organization and not just from facilities' perspective.

Other functions that may want be involved in the renegotiation process include legal and finance. Legal has the responsibility to make sure that new terms are legal, and that the organization can stay compliant within that framework. Additionally, legal has to make sure that the organization is not entering a binding agreement that is illegal. Functions such as finance would want to make sure that fees associated with any changes are tracked and accounted for. In order to keep the process moving, the project manager for contract rene-gotiations should adapt and adjust the teams and processes to meet their organization's requirements to procure new contracts.

It goes without saying that most vendors have quotas and time constraints in getting deals booked. When negotiating, always keep the timing of meeting dates in the back of your mind as it gets close to the end to the year, quarter, or month. In cases where the negotiation may impact the contract price negatively, the vendor may opt to make changes after the first of the year. The important requirement for any negotiator is to be aware and flexible when looking for opportunities.

When negotiating vendor contracts, make sure that both your team and the vendor representatives have the authority to negotiate. It is very disappointing to find out after the fact that either your team or the vendor representative has to go back to another person to sell the changes. This delays the process and doubles the negotiations by requiring multiple approval levels before a transaction can be implemented.

The working group should provide a deadline for the initiative, so as to not prolong the process and keep the process moving. Typically a 90-day window is perfect for capturing high-value contract opportunities. In the first 30 days, the team can identify all the targeted contracts, form the teams, and begin setting up appointments with the vendors. By 60 days, most of the vendor meetings should be completed, with some results posted. This phase includes at least two or three appointments with each vendor, with some confidence in knowing if the negotiations are going to yield any fruit. By day 90, the conversations should be put on paper and sent to legal and finance for review. Additionally, all the financial impacts should be calculated and documented.

Although vendors make promises, the agreement has to be put on paper and executed to go into effect. Often the working team walks away from the meeting after the handshake only to realize that nothing was executed. The vendor has no incentive to make the changes that will eventually reduce their fees. Even after execution, it is critical that the department manager or the MM leader review the accounts payable to make sure the vendor is in compliance with the new terms of the contract. It is amazing how often the vendor still charges you the higher rates, even after renegotiation. The project coordinator needs to keep the team on task and make sure that all contracts have been processed and executed.

The contract working group should spend a significant amount of time reviewing contracts for effectiveness and value. Contracts that have been outdated or do not provide any more value for the organization should be terminated immediately. Typical areas that see outdated contracts are predominantly IT contracts. As new systems come online, old systems are kept for a duration after go-live and often forgotten about. A good place to start is to ask for an accounts payable list of vendor payments and find out what is being paid and why. The vendor has no incentive to let you know that the contract is not being used. The entire responsibility falls on the organization to manage the contracts.

Healthcare organizations inevitably have to manage provider contracts. This includes many provider contracts in such areas as emergency medicine, hospitals, anesthesia, radiologists, and on-call providers. As the organization changes over time, it is important to review provider contracts to make sure they are compliant with all the terms. This includes financial and other quality and service terms within the contract. This function should be managed by the chief medical officer (CMO) of the organization and his or her team.

Other provider contracts that require routine scrutiny are partnerships and joint ventures with outside provider and group practices. It is amazing how quickly unmonitored agreements fall out of compliance with the original objectives and goals. In any provider agreement, the value of the partnership has to be routinely measured on a quarterly basis. Joint ventures that were based on increased volumes have to be measured and evaluated for efficacy.

High-performing organizations utilize powerful technology tools to manage contracts consistently. This includes systems that have the ability to compile all the contracts in an organization. Additionally, these systems have robust decision-support alerts that notify contract owner of critical dates such as "notification dates." Technology tools are also able to create reports that show consolidation opportunities. Many vendors contract out various products in multiple departments individually. These contract systems are able to identify opportunities to consolidate and gain economies of scale for better terms.

Although technology is a significant tool that should be utilized in managing contracts, it is no substitute for having a team that consistently goes through contracts on an annual basis. The organization, just like its vendors, are in a constant state of change. Contracts that were required today may be obsolete tomorrow. Vendors may have put obscure clauses in the contract that can raise rates or put you out of compliance, triggering significant penalties.

Putting a robust program in place to manage all enterprise contracts can be done in less than 100 days. Exhibit 11.2 shows a potential timeline for implementation for an enterprise-wide contracts management program.

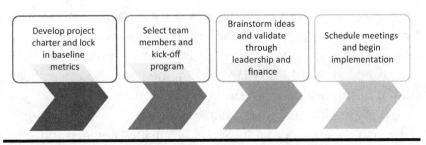

Exhibit 11.2   The contract program 100-day roll out plan.

Step 1 is for the senior leadership to develop a project charter with scope, timelines, resources, and targets expectations. Once the PM is identified, an assessment of existing systems and processes must be completed. Based on findings metrics have to be developed and baselines locked in.

Step 2: Senior leadership in conjunction with the PM must identify working group membership. The CEO should bring the team together and explain the charter objectives and expectations. Additionally, in this step a contract management office has to be funded to assist once the initiative is complete for sustainability purposes.

Step 3: In this step of the process, the working group should review resources and processes required to complete the objective. The working group has an opportunity to bring in new members, identify new metrics, and verify the opportunity. Additionally, the working group has the opportunity to identify new tools, and processes to enhance contract management across the enterprise.

Step 4: The Pm or project coordinator must kick-start the program by setting up the initial team meetings. This includes the routine working group meetings, meetings with operators, and vendor negotiation meetings.

The return on this investment is significant since a 1% improvement in most organizations can represent millions in opportunity. Additionally, benefits from contract changes can be realized much quicker than from most other initiatives. It is for these reasons, that it is critical for every organization to have a robust contract management team in place for a perpetual review of contracts.

Closing: Your Organization Is Only 100 Days Away from High Performance

By failing to prepare, you are preparing to fail.

Benjamin Franklin

Your organization is only 100 days away from kicking off its journey to high performance. All it takes is a vision of a brighter future, the will to change, and the fortitude to hold those around you accountable. The task required to get to a high-performance state within your organization is tactical in nature and there is precedence. The difficulty is in deciding to start the journey and mobilizing the organization.

The journey begins with understanding the forces that are driving the healthcare industry. Moving faster than ever before, the industry will continue to experience significant pressures from consumers, competitors, payors, and government forces. These forces will make the landscape unpredictable, unstable, and tumultuous as we move into the next decade. Organizations that are nimble and have a high-performance infrastructure in place will thrive. Those that depend on past business models and old systems will find themselves falling behind further and further, year after year.

Key changes that will be required for survival in the new landscape include strengthening leadership alignment, creating a robust Performance Improvement (PI) philosophy, designing an expanded project management office (PMO) model, and implementing a governance structure that ensures sustainability. These changes are the ingredients that contribute to a culture of change, revenue growth, expense control, and a sense of accountability that is inherent in every employee within your organization. Organizations that are able to create a new culture of continuous quality improvement that is inherent in everything they do will be ready for any changes that come their way.

Speed is the key for survival in the next decade. All infrastructure changes in the new models and systems must allow the organization to be nimble and able to change quickly with environmental requirements. In any given day, an organization can wake up to find itself without a managed care contract, with a new competitor outside, or facing new changes in governmental regulations. It is the speed at which each organization adapts to these changes that will differentiate the winners from the losers. Senior leadership must develop leaders that can operate autonomously and allow them to make mistakes without retribution.

High-performance organizations developing infrastructure to neutralize anticipated environmental pressures start with strong leadership alignment. This process starts by picking the top leader that exemplifies the characteristics that the organization wants to adopt. The senior leader has to show his/her subordinates the link between the vision, mission, and current gaps in performance. The gaps will lead to strategies and ultimately to outcomes that close the gap to the vision of the organization. This linkage process is critical to aligning all leaders in the direction that the organization is headed in.

A key strategy in leadership alignment for high-performing organizations is to create a close partnership between the chief executive officer (CEO)/chief operating officer (COO), chief financial officer (CFO), and the vice president (VP) of PI. For expense reduction and new revenue initiatives, organizations need to leverage these three skill sets to drive the organization. The CFO typically find gaps in performance, the VP of PI identifies the opportunities and creates teams to drive change, and the CEO/COO ultimately mobilize the organization for outcomes. This synergistic relationship has proven very powerful in high-performing organizations.

The linkage between strategy and tactics is extended from the functional VPs to the project team members completing the alignment loop. This linkage between senior leaders has to extend all the way to the frontline staff doing the project tasks. At every step of the way, all leaders have to know what is being done and why. Additionally, they need to know their role in the process and when they need to act to remove barriers. This alignment model creates a system that is singularly focused on the objectives of the organization and supports a culture of accountability and transparency.

As the leadership alignment linkage is developed, organizations need a strong PI model to help guide the organization toward outcomes. To prepare for the next generation of changes, it is imperative that every organization design and develop a robust PI program. Here are the top 10 strategies that every organization should be considering in developing a high-performance PI function in the coming decade:

1. Bring in the right PI leadership that can envision big results.
2. Ensure PI leaders of the future work closely with system-level COOs and CFOs to produce results.
3. Keep your PI department Lean.
4. Create a permanent organizational governance structure for PI initiatives.

5. Redefine your PMO project life cycle.
6. Focus on 90-day projects that maximize your returns.
7. Make complex information easy to understand and actionable.
8. Equip PI departments with a new breed of staff that can manage the entire project life cycle.
9. If you are going to do Lean Six Sigma training across the enterprise, do it in a meaningful way.
10. Ensure PI programs leverage information and innovations across the enterprise for optimal results.

These recommended modifications in existing PI models will prepare the organization to cope with the imminent changes expected in the next decade. The critical element of this infrastructure requirement is that the PI leader is elevated to the top with strong authority. For this model to work, strong executive-level PI leaders have to be identified and encouraged to work hand in hand with operators and finance to drive the organization.

PI functions need strong tools and methodologies that measure, track, and report on initiatives and projects throughout the organization. Allowing the PI function to redesign the PMO is critical to the implementation of all the associated PI initiatives. Strong PMO structure supports greater speed in decision making and holding leaders accountable. With the development of the Project Management Institute, methodologies have become more consistent and mainstream nationally. But even with these developments, the typical project management models still have weaknesses. This weakness is evident in a recent industry report that indicated a 50% failure rate in healthcare projects. The foundation of this failure is almost always rooted in project support from senior leadership and benefit realization.

The flaw in the existing project life cycle today is that it starts at the point of kick-off and ends at go-live. Although there is an initiating and planning phase in the existing model, it is predominately a function of a project that has already been approved and funded. There is little understanding of the outcomes that are desired and reasons behind the initiative. Additionally, in the existing model, the benefits are almost never calculated in the outcomes that were originally desired after go-live. The success of the project is measured by the ability of the project manager to implement the system or the process.

In this case, the project manager was never aware of all the reasons behind the approval of the project and, additionally, never went back to measure and see if all those assumptions were realized. Although the project was a success in the eyes of the project manager, it was a failure in the eyes of leadership and those that originally approved the project. This situation occurs in about 50% of healthcare projects according to the Gartner Group. This represents billions in waste throughout the industry.

To counter these failure rates, many organizations have started to expand the definition of the project life cycle to include project procurement before kick-off and benefits realization after go-live. In this new expanded model, the project is flanked on either end with procurement and benefits realization. With this change, the culture of the management team begins to shift from go-live to outcomes.

Just like project procurement, benefits realization after a project go-live is critical to a high-performing PMO function. Most leaders typically do not measure success once the project moves past go-live. It is almost always assumed that the benefits will automatically follow. This is a big assumption that is typically not true in healthcare projects, as evident in the current failure rates. It is not until months or often years later that leadership begins asking questions about projects that never materialized the benefits they were expecting. For this reason, no project is over until the benefits of the project have been tallied and the outcomes measured against the original expectations of leadership.

Once the tools are in place, the last leg of the puzzle is the development of the governance infrastructure model for the implementation of change. The secret to my success in delivering bottom-line financial results year after year has always been in developing an A+ governance infrastructure. It took years to understand what this means and to learn that there is more value in building a great system that never stops versus trying to do it all yourself.

Finding the correct strategy in developing a robust governance infrastructure makes all the difference between organizations that can never find their way to results and those that see them every day. A common disappointment in the last two decades has been the sustainability of programs. Part of the solution is building a great infrastructure that controls output regularly. The basis of this model is rooted in the continuous quality improvement (CQI) concepts of the 1980s.

In this CQI model, looking for new opportunities to improve becomes ingrained into the day-to-day activities of the employees. It slowly morphs the organizational culture into one that is constantly looking for ways to improve. In preparing for the semi-annual brainstorming sessions, many team members and leads begin accumulating ideas months before. This manifestation of the governance and infrastructure is the cornerstone of creating a culture that sustains programs through the CQI model.

Developing an A+ governance infrastructure in an organization to implement changes is not difficult, although it does require compliance with 10 crucial steps:

1. Identifying and developing the sponsor
2. Identifying and developing the project manager
3. Creating a steering committee
4. Creating a working group
5. Creating team leads
6. Creating team members

7. Reporting functions
8. Scheduling all the meetings
9. Creating the project coordinator
10. Documenting the meeting and sending out notes

Once the infrastructure is in place, the organization is ready to mobilize. A select group of leaders led by the CEO/CFO/PI should identify the leaders that will lead the CQI initiatives across the enterprise. Although organizations may have PI initiatives that are focused on quality or service, the focus of this book is on expense reduction and revenue enhancement opportunities.

Based on a typical healthcare facility's cost structure, there are several levers that are consistently used to control expense and improve revenues. These include non-labor expense control, labor management, contracts management, length of stay (LOS) management, and revenue cycle improvement. LOS is a special area of opportunity as it can impact both labor and supplies at the same time but requires significant clinician involvement.

Non-Labor

As the name implies, non-labor is basically all projects that are not related to labor. Typically, these projects include supply chain management, product line vendor management, the utilization of products by providers, and technology resources. Although non-labor can be defined very broadly as an expense reduction strategy, in most organizations it does not include initiatives such as new revenue opportunities, revenue cycle optimization, patient access, and LOS. The advantage of non-labor is that it is often the easiest to pursue as it does not impact employees. Prioritizing non-labor projects as a source of expense reduction is also in complete alignment with the mission ethics of religious-based organizations.

Organizations can enjoy huge returns in non-labor expense reduction by following several key steps that have over time proven instrumental. These include identifying and measuring the correct key performance indicators, setting up a strong governance structure, and finally assigning top leadership to ensure success. The final step and the most critical is accountability. The CEO is responsible for driving the leaders. Without accountability the entire process will fall short. So when mid-level directors and employees test the resolve of the governance process, the leadership should be swift in guiding the team members.

The most important aspect of rolling out non-labor within any organization is educating the teams about how this is a CQI process that will last in perpetuity. Team members and projects may change over time, but the committee will identify new opportunities every 6 months and continue the process indefinitely. This will ensure the sustainability of the program across the enterprise.

Labor

Labor costs represent more than 50% of the annual budget in most hospitals in the US health system. This opportunity is growing based on recent increases in minimum wage and premium pay standards. Additionally, with the advent of the Affordable Care Act and baby boomers gearing for retirement, labor costs are expected to increase. To survive the next decade, organizations have to develop strategies that deploy the workforce in the most efficient and productive manner for long-term sustainability. Unfortunately, labor is not easy to control. There are union, city, state, and federal regulations to contend with, as well as market forces and organizational culture. Organizations that are able to navigate these barriers and design innovative labor management models will be poised for success. This chapter will provide a practical approach to managing labor in your facility.

Managing labor is a large-scale endeavor, and the best approach is to employ the PI model which breaks labor systems into technology, people, and processes. Technology represents the information management systems and tools that assist with functions such as benchmarking, staff scheduling, reporting, forecasting, budgeting, and calculating labor statistics. People represents the human factor of labor management and includes activities such as developing work standards, pay scales, benefits, licensing, and staffing to volumes. Managing labor processes refers to procedures that control the procurement and management of human resources. This includes factors such as full-time equivalent approval and managing outlier staffing processes.

Length of Stay

LOS is growing in importance as a strategic approach to treating the root of the problem versus the symptoms of expense reduction. For decades, healthcare administrators have approached expense reduction strategies from a traditional business management model. This includes the strong management of resources such as labor, non-labor, portfolio review, contracts, and supply chain. Unfortunately, this has left 80% of current healthcare expenses untouched as the utilization of care is under the control of the providers. Because of misaligned incentives between physicians and hospitals, it has been common knowledge for years that approximately 30% of services in acute care facilities are medically unnecessary. The ability to control the medical management of patients is the newest frontier in expense reduction in healthcare and holds significant promise in reducing the costs of treating patients while increasing quality and service.

Although the medical management of patients can come in many forms, the three main areas that hold the most opportunity are order set utilization, clinical pathways, and LOS management. In the provider utilization model, a simple change in the patient treatment pattern can impact all expense categories. For example, in LOS, if a patient leaves in 5 days instead of 7, less labor, tests, drugs, images, and therapies are required. Additionally, for organizations struggling with capacity issues, this model can be used to create artificial capacity. LOS ultimately impacts every category of operations and expenses; hence, many administrators firmly believe that the biggest opportunity in the coming decade for operational optimization and expense reduction is in medical management.

The management of clinical utilization is ripe with opportunity, and requires significant provider involvement. As only physicians can write the orders for admission, treatment, and discharge, they have significant control over the treatment options for a patient. Partnering with providers to identify best practices for clinical pathways or LOS is not just a good thing, it's a requirement. And providers for the most part have been open to working with administrators to develop mutual solutions. As an increasing number of providers turn to the employment model, the ability to reduce variation and the opportunity for efficiency increases significantly. Physician-owned models typically have the highest quality, service, and efficiency outcomes and are in the best position to manage clinical utilization.

Access

Access to healthcare is one of the most fundamental aspects of keeping a community healthy and maximizing the utilization of organizational assets. In many organizations, there are artificial barriers at every point of entry into the system that prevent patients from getting basic care such as primary, specialty, ancillary, emergency, and surgical services. This inability to get patients into the system has adverse effects on both the community and profit margins. Identifying and implementing strategies that improve access to care will improve the health and well-being of communities and organizations' margins. As there are many variables that impact access, the focus of this book has been on logistical processes such as scheduling, precertifications, and physician access.

To improve access, leadership needs to remove every barrier between the patients and the services being provided by the system. To identify and understand the opportunities for improvement, organizations have to employee PI services to map critical processes such as scheduling, precertification, and emergency room services. Additionally, key metrics have to be gathered for functions such as patient placement, transfers, days out to service, and registration for analysis and evaluation. This information combined can begin painting a picture of the opportunities that can facilitate access to healthcare.

Although access comprises many factors such as insurance, money, location, and information, the four chief areas of opportunity in access for healthcare organizations include provider appointment, emergency services, post-acute, and surgical access. These four services together represent 90% of the patient experience in the acute care setting. Managing access to these services can have the largest impact, one that can be measured in the millions.

Revenue Cycle

This is an area of tremendous opportunity in most organizations. The right revenue cycle leader can bring millions of dollars of opportunity to the organization. It is estimated that up to 25% of bills are rejected by CMS and more than 50% of those are never refiled. This represents a significant loss of revenues from improper billing. Optimizing revenue cycle efficiency and improving the areas of medical billing, coding, and accounts receivable management are critical in staying financially viable in the next decade.

According to the Healthcare Financial Management Association, the revenue cycle process includes all the administrative and clinical functions that contribute to the capture, management, and collection of patient service revenue.

Based on this definition, the process begins at the point when a patient account is created and ends at the point when the balance has been satisfied.

Hospital revenue cycle systems include both clinical and administrative functions related to the generation, management, and collection of patient care revenue. In the past, these functions were often referred to as back-end functions such as billing and collections. Today the system is focused on both the back end and the front end, including patient scheduling and registration, insurance verification, and preauthorization, as well as the core tasks of the revenue cycle including medical documentation and coding.

Contracts

Vendor contracts represent about a quarter of a typical healthcare facility's expense structure. A 500-bed hospital in the United States may have as much as $100 million in contracts paid out annually. These include supply chain contracts, consulting services, maintenance agreements, construction contracts, and purchase services. Many organizations target contracts as a priority for expense reduction because they are considered an easier opportunity to go after in comparison to areas such as labor or clinical variation. Additionally, the impact is felt much quicker than most other expense reduction initiatives. Any organization serious about staying ahead of the expense reduction curve should have a robust program that manages contracts through a CQI approach.

The contract working group should have a target that they are planning to achieve by renegotiating and eliminating contracts. From a PI perspective, most organizations tend to achieve a 5% opportunity based on various factors. So if an organization has targeted $100 million worth of contracts, the teams should be targeting $5 million in opportunity or 5% of each contract. At first glance, this may be an insurmountable task but there are many reasons why these targets are achievable. For example, contract management can also mean contract termination, which can have a significant impact on your overall spend. So, although some vendors may not negotiate, others will and if you cancel a few contracts the total amount goes toward your target.

Any healthcare organization that can bring in a strong infrastructure and take control of these initiatives will find itself at the head of the pack in short order. In 100 days, your organization could be on its journey to a healthy bottom line with improved quality and service across the enterprise. By following the step-by-step process in this book, your organization is assured a place at the head of the pack by creating a culture of improvement, accountability, and peak performance.

Index

Turnaround times (TAT) reports,
97–98
Turnkey systems, 115

Units of service, 78
Up-front collections, 121

Vendor contracts, 13, 129–139,
152–153
Vice president (VP), 57, 82, 126

Vision statements, 18
VP. *see* Vice president (VP)

Weekend differential, 79
Worked hours per unit of
service, 78
Work force optimization, 87
Working group, 56, 100, 113
leaders, 131
Working team, 100

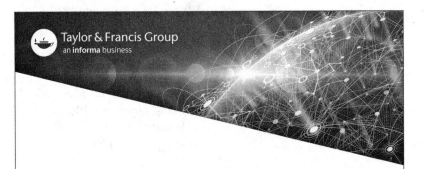